LIBERATION

Stories of Survival From the Holocaust

The Holocaust Through Primary Sources

Betty N. Hoffman

Enslow Publishers, Inc.
40 Industrial Road
Box 398
Berkeley Heights, NJ 07922
USA

http://www.enslow.com

To my family

Library of Congress Cataloging-in-Publication Data

Hoffman, Betty N.

    Liberation : stories of survival from the Holocaust / Betty N. Hoffman.

       p. cm. — (The Holocaust through primary sources)

    Summary: "Discusses the liberation of Europe and the aftermath of the Holocaust, including the displaced persons camps, primary source accounts from Holocaust survivors, and how those survivors started new lives in new countries"—Provided by publisher.

    Includes bibliographical references and index.

    ISBN 978-0-7660-3319-1

    1. Holocaust, Jewish (1939–1945)—Personal narratives—Juvenile literature. 2. Holocaust survivors—Biography—Juvenile literature. 3. Jews—Europe—Biography—Juvenile literature. 4. Jewish refugees—Europe—Biography—Juvenile literature. 5. Immigrants—Biography—Juvenile literature. 6. World War, 1939–1945—Refugees—Europe—Juvenile literature. 7. World War, 1939–1945—Europe—End—Juvenile literature. I. Title.

    D804.195.H64 2011

    940.53'180922—dc22   2010007234

Paperback ISBN 978-1-59845-348-5

Printed in China

10 9 8 7 6 5 4 3 2 1

052011 Leo Paper Group, Heshan City, Guangdong, China

To Our Readers: We have done our best to make sure all Internet Addresses in this book were active and appropriate when we went to press. However, the author and the publisher have no control over and assume no liability for the material available on those Internet sites or on other Web sites they may link to. Any comments or suggestions can be sent by e-mail to comments@enslow.com or to the address on the back cover.

Every effort has been made to locate all copyright holders of material used in this book. If any errors or omissions have occurred, please contact us at www.enslow.com. We will try to make corrections in future editions.

Illustration Credits: © akg-images / The Image Works, p. 12; Associated Press, p. 40; Courtesy of the Bloomfield Journal, pp. 95, 104; Central Zionist Archives, p. 31; Courtesy of Dora Rytman, pp. 61, 68; Enslow Publishers, Inc., p. 10; Courtesy of Henry Levy, pp. 82, 93; Courtesy of Philip and Ruth Rabinowitz Lazowski, pp. 73, 77, 79; © Photo12 / The Image Works, p. 89; Courtesy of Roza Lundina and Naum Gupper, pp. 44, 46, 47; ullstein bild / The Granger Collection, New York, p. 8; USHMM, p. 52; USHMM, courtesy of Alex Hochhauser, p. 113; USHMM, courtesy of American Jewish Joint Distribution Committee, p. 33; USHMM, courtesy of Avi Livney, p. 111; USHMM, courtesy of David Sion, p. 84; USHMM, courtesy of Dr. Mark Liwszyc, p. 59; USHMM, courtesy of Elaine Frank, p. 99; USHMM, courtesy of George Kadish / Zvi Kadushin, p. 37; USHMM, courtesy of Irene Rogers, p. 75; USHMM, courtesy of Jack Sutin, p. 109; USHMM, courtesy of Joe Yablon, p. 6; USHMM, courtesy of Leah Lahav, p. 66; USHMM, courtesy of Lev Sviridov, p. 19; USHMM, courtesy of Marc Block, p. 37 (top); USHMM, courtesy of Mayer and Rachel Abramowitz, p. 55; USHMM, courtesy of Menachem Galon, p. 112; USHMM, courtesy of Miriam Kushelewicz Levitt, p. 57; USHMM, courtesy of National Archives and Records Administration, pp. 15, 26, 29; USHMM, courtesy of Sam and Helen Bronner, p. 71; USHMM, courtesy of Samuel and Ala Brand, p. 92; USHMM, courtesy of Walter Greenberg, p. 97; USHMM, courtesy of Yad Vashem, p. 87; U.S. National Archives, p. 103; Courtesy of the Zeeberg Family, p. 50; Courtesy of the Zukerman-Fish-Wyner Family, pp. 17, 22, 23.

Cover Illustration: USHMM, courtesy of National Archives and Records Administration (Jewish women and children in Auschwitz after the camp's liberation in January 1945); USHMM, courtesy of Fritz Gluckstein (Star of David artifact).

Contents

INTRODUCTION

> "With all due respect to the most sensitive and learned of historians, I feel that only those of us who were its victims can give credence to its horrors."
>
> —Henry Levy[1]

As World War II wore on in the spring of 1945, the prisoners in the Buchenwald concentration camp in Germany were starved and weary. On April 8, 1945, the Nazis forced thousands of them to march away from the camp. The Nazi guards left many behind. None of the prisoners knew if they would live or die.

Three days later, American soldiers liberated Buchenwald. Hayim-Meir Gottlieb, a young survivor, wrote in his diary:

> Then came April 11. Liberation. An American commander took over the camp. . . . Gradually the inmates of Buchenwald began to live again. Once apathetic and hopeless, they now nearly went mad with joy. Freedom! Freedom! We lived to see it.

Where now? Where to? Things are not so simple. To go back to Poland? To Hungary? To streets empty of Jews, towns empty of Jews, a world without Jews. To wander in those lands, lonely, homeless, always with the tragedy before one's eyes . . . and to meet again a former Gentile neighbor who would open his eyes wide and smile, remarking with double meaning, "What! You're still alive!" . . . We now understood that our situation was different from all others in the camp. For us there was no going back where we came from.[2]

Adolf Hitler, Chancellor of Germany

In 1932, the National Socialist German Workers' Party, also called the Nazi Party, won more votes in the *Reichstag* (German Parliament) elections than any other political party. This made Adolf Hitler the leader of the most powerful political party in Germany. Although Hitler lost the presidential election to General Paul von Hindenburg that year, he was appointed chancellor of Germany in 1933. When Hindenburg died in 1934, Hitler took control of the government and became dictator.

Hitler hated the Jews and used them as a scapegoat for the problems in Germany. He saw Jews as subhuman. Hatred of Jews—just because they are Jews—is called antisemitism. Antisemitism can lead to persecution. Hitler's antisemitism led to mass murder.

Other people the Nazis did not want in the new Germany were the Roma and Sinti (previously called "Gypsies") and citizens of some countries, such as Poland and the Soviet Union. They also excluded those with different political views, religions, or behaviors, such as Communists, Jehovah's Witnesses, and homosexuals.

The First Days of War

In August 1939, Germany and the Soviet Union signed a secret agreement not to fight each other. They planned to take over several countries, including Poland.

World War II officially began on September 1, 1939, when Germany invaded Poland. Within weeks, Germany and the Soviet Union conquered and divided Poland between them.

Three young survivors at the Buchenwald concentration camp in Germany pose smiling for their American liberators. Many survivors, like Hayim-Meir Gottlieb, were overjoyed with their freedom, but were not sure where they would go to start a new life.

Less than two years later, on June 22, 1941, the Germans broke their promise and attacked the Soviet Union. The war spread around the globe. On December 7, 1941, Germany's ally Japan attacked Pearl Harbor in Hawaii. The next day, American President Franklin D. Roosevelt declared war on Japan and, on December 11, he declared war on Germany.

The Holocaust

Millions of people were victims of the Nazis. However, a larger percentage of the Jewish population was tortured and killed than any other group. Of an estimated 15.3 million Jews worldwide in 1933, about 9.5 million lived in Europe. The Nazis murdered about 6 million of them.

The Nazis forced many Jews into ghettos—run-down Jewish neighborhoods kept separate from the rest of the population. This made it easier for the Germans to steal the Jews' possessions, force them to work, or kill them. The living areas in the ghettos were cramped and dirty. Jews were forced to do brutal work. They never had enough food. Nazis with guns and dogs watched the Jews and kept them from escaping. Many died in the ghettos. Residents of the ghettos would eventually be transported by train to the forced labor and death camps.

In January 1942, high-ranking Nazi officials met in Berlin to discuss the "final solution" to the Jewish problem. They discussed their plan for the total annihilation of Europe's Jews. However, this had already begun in the Soviet Union where killing squads marched Jews to nearby forests or fields and killed them. In other towns, they simply took Jews to the edge of town and shot them, pushing their bodies into mass graves.

Between 1932 and 1945, the Nazis organized about twenty thousand concentration camps. Some of these were transit camps where the Nazis gathered people before sending them to work camps or death camps. Even though the work camps were not specifically death camps, many died there from overwork, starvation, disease, and murder.

The purpose of the death camps was to murder all Jews and others from the so-called "subhuman" races. The Nazis built gas chambers to kill large groups efficiently. During the worst years, the Nazis gassed as many as six thousand Jews a day at Auschwitz-Birkenau. By the end of the war, more than 3 million Jews had died in the death camps.

A German tank convoy passes through an unidentified Russian town in the fall of 1941. The Germans broke their agreement with the Soviet Union and invaded the country on June 22, 1941.

In many places, Christian families stayed in their villages after the Germans occupied their countries. But Jews could not. To avoid capture, some hid in the forests. But it was very difficult for Jews to fight back. They had few weapons. They knew that if they protested or resisted, the Germans would kill many innocent people in response.

Nevertheless, Jews, when they could, joined the armies in their countries. Others fought in the forests as partisans—members of small groups that attacked the Germans in occupied areas. Some of the non-Jewish partisan groups were also antisemitic. They refused to admit Jews and sometimes killed them. Others allowed Jews to join but discriminated against them. Some Jews formed their own partisan units, which fought bravely and protected those who could not fight.[3]

Liberation

In April 1945, Dwight D. Eisenhower, General of the Army, commanded all of the soldiers in the Allied armies that had fought against the Germans. On May 7, 1945, German General Alfred Jodl surrendered to Eisenhower, ending the war with Germany.

Many of the Jewish survivors had lived through the brutality and murder of the ghettos and concentration camps. Others had hidden wherever they could. Some were saved by courageous Christians. In other places, Christian neighbors had been too afraid to help the Jews or had joined the Nazis in robbing and murdering them.

The Liberation of Major Nazi Camps

- ○ Liberated by the United States
- ○ Liberated by Great Britain/Canada
- ● Liberated by the Soviet Union
- Territory Liberated Prior to March 21, 1945
- Territory Liberated March 21—May 7–9, 1945
- Territory Held by Germany at Surrender May 7–9, 1945
- Surrender May 7–9, 1945

0   50 Miles
0   50KM

DENMARK

North Sea

Stutthof
May 1945

N
W   E
S

Neungamme
May 1945

Woebbelin
May 1945

Westerbork
April 1945

Ravensbrück
April 1945

Vistula

Bergen-Belsen
April 1945

Salzwedel
April 1945

Sachsenhausen
April 1945

GREATER GERMANY

EASTERN FRONT
April 1945

Dora-Mittelbau
April 1945

Buchenwald
April 1945

Elbe

Gross-Rosen
February 1945

Majdanek
July 1944

Rhine

Ohrdruf
April 1945

Theresienstadt
Ghetto

Oder

Flossenbürg
April 1945

PROTECTORATE
OF BOHEMIA
AND MORAVIA

Auschwitz
January 1945

FRANCE

WESTERN FRONT
April 1945

SLOVAKIA

Danube

Gusen May 1945
Mauthausen May 1945

Dachau
April 1945

Gunskirchen
May 1945

HUNGARY

Landsberg
April 1945

Ebensee
May 1945

SWITZERLAND

As the Allied forces swept across Europe defeating the German army, they started to liberate the Nazi camps. Soviet forces liberated the first major Nazi camp in July 1944. This map shows all the camps and territory liberated by the Allies.

Millions of non-Jews who had left their homes because of the war were eager to go home. But many Jews had no home. Although Jews had lived in Europe for many generations, many countries did not accept them as part of the general population. With their distinct religion, culture, and languages, the Jews were clearly identifiable and were often discriminated against.

No Country of Their Own

The problem, according to one group of Jews, called Zionists, was that they did not have a country of their own. But they did have a historic homeland. It is written in the Bible that God gave the Jews the land of Israel, which they ruled for many years. Eventually, stronger groups conquered the Jewish country. Even though the Jews did not have a Jewish-led government in the Holy Land, some Jews had always lived there. Those who lived elsewhere remembered their national past and prayed to return.

In the late 1800s, small groups of Jews began to return to the Holy Land. They bought land from the Arabs and built farms and homes. After World War I, the League of Nations asked the British to supervise the Holy Land. This was called the British Mandate for Palestine. Neither the British nor the Arabs, who also had a history in Palestine, wanted more Jews to settle there.

In the 1930s, the British Mandate government refused to admit many Jewish refugees from Hitler's Germany. In 1938, the British issued a document called a White Paper, which limited Jewish immigration even further. But some Jews, who had no place to go to escape antisemitism, entered the country illegally.

German Jews stand in line outside the Palestine and Orient Travel Agency in Berlin, Germany, on January 22, 1939, trying to emigrate to Palestine. After the British issued a White Paper in 1938, immigration to Palestine became especially difficult for Jews trying to escape antisemitism in Nazi Germany.

The Jewish Agency was the unofficial Jewish government in Palestine. It organized Jewish life, worked with the British Mandate government, and supervised the illegal immigration from Europe. The Jewish Agency planned to transform the British Mandate in Palestine into a Jewish nation that welcomed all Jews who needed a home. After the Holocaust, the Jews needed a new home, but they had few places to turn.

1 The Zukerman Family

As the American army and its allies moved into Germany and German-occupied countries like Poland, they found the concentration camps. American John Faitella, a military policeman in General Patton's Third Army, patrolled the areas in a jeep. His group looked for German soldiers. Faitella has never forgotten seeing Buchenwald, a concentration camp in Germany:

> We went into this camp. There was nobody around, no German soldiers, no American soldiers. The first thing I saw was a gate wide open and a big, high fence, really high. As you entered on the right, there was a fence with these German police dogs and Doberman pinchers, the red and black ones. They were rough dogs.
>
> The barracks were maybe 60 feet by . . . 100-150 feet. The beds were just wooden planks. There were maybe six or seven men on each tier. Some couldn't move. The three of us started in the front door there. Oh, my God, the smell, the stink!

Around the back was where I seen the furnaces and about 20 to 25 feet away from the furnace, a nice little pile of ashes, say, 20 to 30 inches high. Further back a little bit, there were bodies, women, and men, stacked like cordwood.

There were two factories there. One was where they made tools, all automobile tools, wrenches, this and that. And the other, they made clothing, uniforms for the German army. So maybe these prisoners worked. But when they couldn't work no more, they let them die.

When I went back to this little town, one lady spoke English. I said, "You mean to tell me you didn't know this camp was up there."

She looked around so nobody would hear. "Yes, but if we'd have said something, even being German, we'd be in there."[1]

John Faitella did not know why the woman said this. Was it because it was true, or because she did not want the Americans to blame her for not helping the prisoners?

The Survivors

The soldiers did not know what to do; neither did the former prisoners. The survivors had lived through such terrible times that

A Jewish survivor at Buchenwald shows American troops the electrified barbed-wire fence at the camp. American soldiers were often stunned by the terrible and brutal conditions at the Nazi camps.

many could not believe they were free. They were starving for food and for news of those they had lost.

About 200,000 Jews were liberated from all the Nazi camps.[2] Of these, about 65,000 were from Poland. Most did not want to return. The Jews from Hungary, Czechoslovakia, and Romania wanted to go home. They believed they might find their families alive. They hoped to make new lives in their old countries. But for many, this did not happen. Their families and communities had been destroyed. Others refused to live in places where people still hated Jews.

The Germans had occupied most of Western Europe. In each country, some people had helped the Nazis. Even so, the situation for Jews had been slightly better there than in Eastern Europe. Denmark—the only country to do so—rescued most of its Jews. Overall, Western European Jews could return to their countries if they chose. No matter where the Jews were from, they wanted to find their families. They wrote letters to everyone they knew asking for news.

Adi, Greta, Nusha, and Debora

The Zukerman family from the Hague, a city in Holland, had been unbelievably lucky. They had been prisoners in two concentration camps: Westerbork and Bergen-Belsen. The younger daughter, Debora, said:

> It was a miracle. We were one of the very few families that came out as a family. My father scrounged around for food to keep us alive. We stayed with my mother, my sister and I. My father stayed in a different part of the camp. My father was the most honest person you would ever want to meet. He wouldn't cheat you out of a penny. During the war, he did anything and everything to keep us alive. He cheated. He stole. Once we were out of camp, it was back to normal life.[3]

Adi and Greta Zukerman at their wedding in the late 1930s in the Hague, a city in Holland. The Zukerman family was very lucky as they were able to stay together throughout the war.

Adi's Letter

Early in the war, the Red Cross had helped Debora Zukerman's father, Adi, send a few letters to his family in Palestine. After that, they heard nothing from each other until Adi Zukerman sent this letter:

> *The Hague: July 19, 1945*
>
> *Dearest Mama, Lotte, Nunio,*
> *and all our family members,*
>
> *We have had to undergo a very terrible time. After I, with still other comrades, had been abused by the SS in the Hague for various work such as cleaning the*

> *barracks, Greta, Nusha, Debora (she was hardly three months old), and I were taken from our home by the SS at midnight on September 29, 1943 and transported to the Dutch transit camp in Westerbork.*

The SS—*Schutzstaffel* (Protection Squadrons)—killed or removed anyone or any group that the Nazis did not like from Nazi-occupied areas.

The Zukermans were among the last Jewish families to be deported from the Hague. Everyone they knew, including Greta's family, was already gone. Nobody knew where the SS had sent them.

Greta Zukerman and both children became very sick in Westerbork and were treated in the camp hospital. As bad as Westerbork was, their next camp, Bergen-Belsen, was worse—even though the family stayed together. Adi's job as a mason was very difficult. Greta took care of the children, who were sick much of the time. Both parents were terribly afraid for their family. Adi Zukerman remembered Bergen-Belsen as "a period of mental and physical tortures. . . . The unshakable will to be preserved for my wife and children helped me over this time."

Liberation

By 1945, Adi Zukerman, like many other Jews, knew that being locked in a cattle car on a train was probably a death sentence. He wrote in the letter:

At Bergen-Belsen, both of the Zukerman children were very sick. Conditions at the camp were deplorable. These female prisoners lie in bunks in the barracks at Bergen-Belsen shortly after the camp was liberated.

On April 10, 1945, we were dragged into cattle cars by the SS. We had to undergo the most terrible hygienic conditions and worrisome hunger. Greta was very sick with typhus. Often I thought that I was to lose the mother of my fervently loved children. The SS had managed to bring us 700 to 800 kilometers deep into Germany near Dresden with the ultimate aim of gassing.

But the Higher Power which up to that point had shielded our way from the worst also protected us in that period. The 23rd of April 1945, the day of our liberation by the Russian Red Army, will forever remain in our memory.

We had to move on instructions from the Russians into houses abandoned by the Germans. I was overcome by the terrible typhus. Nusha also became the victim of that disease. But the Good Spirit, which had accompanied us on our paths in the time of horror, did not abandon us that time either.

All starved to the bones, we were treated and provided for first class by the Russians. Then, we were sent to Holland on June 21, 1945, in an American hospital train.

There, after a few weeks of quarantine, we were admitted into the Hague on the 14th of July.

I am one of the richest of men. My whole family lives. Alas, of the farther family only Ester and Klara Blok and Lida Poons with her husband and child survived. Ester was in Auschwitz. Klara, Lida, and family had gone into hiding.

We must learn to forget the past and to direct our eyes to the future. I am very thin, but I have already started on the way to improvement. White hair decorates my head. The children were cut completely bald. However, I am satisfied in every way with the appearance of Greta and the children.

My nice furniture, my home I have lost. But I am a billionaire. My wife and children have been preserved for me. I live in the store of Mr. Blok, which Klara Blok runs at the moment. Klara, Ester, a young woman from Vienna, and us all form a community.

The times have hardened us, but my warm heart still beats not only for my family, no, also for my only mother, sister, and brother.

Your, Adi[4]

Adi Zukerman sent this letter to his mother on July 19, 1945.

Zukerman thought that it would take him only a year to leave Holland and go to the United States, but it took much longer. First, he had to find a sponsor, a relative to invite the family to the United States. Then he had to find a job and a place to live.

It took until 1953 for the Zukermans to arrive in Connecticut. During the first months, Adi Zukerman's distant relatives, the Rosensteins, shared their home with the family. They also gave Zukerman a job as an accountant in their store.

Adi Zukerman's health was not good. He was a heavy smoker, and his terrible experiences in the concentration camps had weakened him. He died in 1956. His wife, Greta, found a job as a secretary, and the girls—Nusha and Debora—grew up as American children.

In this photo taken after the war, Adi and Greta Zukerman pose with their daughters, Nusha (left) and Debora. The family stayed in Holland until 1953, waiting for permission to go to the United States.

On April 12, 1945, General Dwight D. Eisenhower, supreme commander of the Allied forces in Europe, saw what he called the "indescribable horror" of the Nazi camps.

Ohrdruf, part of Buchenwald, was the first Nazi concentration camp liberated by American soldiers. The prisoners at Ohrdruf were forced laborers. Their main project was to build a railway. What Eisenhower saw that day influenced his view of the camp survivors. He wrote:

> I have never felt able to describe my emotional reactions when I first came face to face with indisputable evidence of Nazi brutality and ruthless disregard of every shred of decency . . .
>
> I visited every nook and cranny of the camp because I felt it my duty to be in a position from then on to testify at first hand about these things in case there ever grew up at home the belief or assumption that "the stories of Nazi brutality were just propaganda." Some members of the visiting party were unable to go through the ordeal.

I not only did so but as soon as I returned to Patton's headquarters that evening I sent communications to both Washington and London urging the two governments to send instantly to Germany a random group of newspaper editors and representative groups from the national legislatures. I felt that the evidence should be immediately placed before the American and British publics in a fashion that would leave no room for cynical doubt.[1]

Preparing to Lead

Dwight D. Eisenhower was born in Denison, Texas, in 1890. Two years later, his family moved to Abilene, Kansas. After graduating from high school, Eisenhower went to the United States Military Academy at West Point. When he graduated in 1915, he became an army officer.

In 1926, Eisenhower went to the Command and General Staff School. The next year he attended the Army War College. Over the years, Eisenhower worked with many generals. He learned a great deal about planning for war and managing armies. He would need these skills during World War II.

Immediately before the United States entered the war, Eisenhower served as the Chief of Staff for General Walter Kreuger, commander of the Third Army. He was promoted twice that year, to colonel and then to brigadier. In December 1941, the

General Dwight Eisenhower (center with officer's hat) looks at the charred remains of prisoners who were burned at a railroad track during the Nazi evacuation of the Ohrdruf concentration camp. Eisenhower was shocked by the "indescribable horror" he saw at the camps.

War Department ordered Eisenhower to Washington. At first, he worked in the War Plans Division. Soon, he rose to major general.

In the summer of 1942, the army sent Eisenhower to England. He became the commanding general in Europe. Six months later, he was named the commander in chief of the Allied forces in North Africa.[2] His next promotion was to supreme commander of the Allied Expeditionary forces in Europe. Now Eisenhower was responsible for the invasion of France—an important part of the plan to defeat Germany.

From D-Day to Victory

On D-Day—June 6, 1944—the first Allied soldiers crossed the English Channel and landed in Normandy, France. Their goal was to connect with the Allied troops in Italy, Eastern Europe, and France. Together, they would crush the Germans. However, the Germans were fierce fighters, and the battles were difficult.

By the end of April 1945, Nazi leaders knew that they had lost the war. On April 30, Adolf Hitler committed suicide. On May 7, 1945, Germany surrendered.

The United States, Great Britain, France, and the Soviet Union divided Germany into four zones. Eisenhower became the military governor of the U.S. Occupation Zone. He also had two other jobs. First, he controlled moving soldiers and supplies out of Germany. Some would go to war in the Far East and Japan.[3] Second, he had to solve the problem of the displaced persons (DPs).

Displaced Persons (DPs)

DPs were people who lived outside their home countries because of the war. Most were not Jewish. The Nazis had forced many farmers and laborers to work in German-occupied countries. Some were volunteers who wanted the Germans to win. Others had no choice but to leave their homes and work for the Nazis.

The armies occupying their countries had displaced additional DPs. Most of these were eager to go home. By the fall of 1945, more than 7 million had returned to their homelands.

The remaining DPs were a mixed group. Some knew if they went home, they would be called traitors for helping the Germans.

Others did not want to go back to countries controlled by the Soviet Union. This left about a million DPs in Europe.[4]

Nearly 100,000 of these were Jews.[5] Some had returned home. When they found their families dead and antisemitism still alive, they went back to the DP camps in Germany. Others had refused to return home in the first place.

The Allies set up DP camps in army training schools, apartment buildings, or, worst of all, in former concentration camps. At first, the Allies divided DP camps by country. This did not work for the Jews because some nations had long histories of antisemitism. In those camps, Jewish DPs saw their former camp guards and others who had mistreated them during the war.[6]

Eisenhower, however, would not allow separate camps for Jews. This reminded him of how the Nazis had discriminated against them. Even so, he realized that the Jewish DPs were different. He wrote:

> Of these DPs the Jews were in the most deplorable condition. For years they had been beaten, starved, and tortured. Even food, clothes, and decent treatment could not immediately enable them to shake off their hopelessness and apathy. . . . To secure for them adequate shelter, to establish a system of food distribution and medical service . . . decent sanitary facilities, heat, and light was a most difficult task.[7]

Overall, it was easier for the army to treat the Jews the same as it did the other DPs.[8] Because some Jewish DPs did not cooperate, the army thought they were difficult. But there were reasons for the way they behaved.

All had suffered terribly. They had lost their families, communities, and their health. A few had small possessions, such as a photograph or two from their previous lives. But most had nothing other than the clothes they wore.

The Jews in the DP camps wanted better food, clothing, housing, jobs, and education. They wanted all-Jewish camps and their own leaders. They refused to go to their home countries.

Jewish DPs wash up in a pool at a displaced persons camp near Hagenow, Germany. Conditions in the DP camps were not always good, and Jewish DPs tried to get better treatment and facilities.

Because no other country would admit them in large numbers, they demanded that the British open Palestine to them.

Then, there were DPs, like Martin Motek Faymann, who refused to go into any camp.[9] According to his daughter, Beatrice Brodie, "He would not go into a DP camp because—he said to me—'If I was behind barbed wire again, I would go crazy.' He could not be subject to anybody else, ever again.'"[10]

The Jewish Brigade

The first Jews that many of the DPs saw were soldiers in the Jewish Brigade of the British army. Most members of the Jewish Brigade were from Palestine. The brigade soldiers wore the Star of David on their uniforms as a badge of honor. The Nazis had forced the Jews to wear this same star. Then, it had marked them as a group deserving of destruction.

Brigade soldiers secretly helped the DPs. They drove brigade trucks to other countries and transported people to Italy and France.[11] They gave DPs food and blankets. They urged them to go to Palestine but warned them that they would have to fight to build a homeland.[12]

The American Army

When the American Jewish soldiers met the DPs, they gave them food and cigarettes—which the DPs used as money. Some soldiers found work for the DPs with the U.S. Army. The Jewish soldiers wrote letters home about the terrible conditions in the DP camps. American newspapers published many of the letters.

Members of the Jewish Brigade tried to help the Jewish DPs.
This is a British recruitment poster encouraging Jews in
Palestine to enlist in the Jewish Brigade in January 1945.

31

Chaplains are religious leaders in the army. It was not their job to help the DPs, but many of them did. One of the first chaplains to arrive, Rabbi Abraham J. Klausner, visited many camps and worked with the DPs. He told the army and Jewish groups what needed to be improved.

Most important, Rabbi Klausner believed the Jewish DPs should be in Jewish camps. He pushed the U.S. Army to transform a Hitler Youth camp into the first all-Jewish camp, Feldafing.[13] The chaplains helped the DPs organize both the individual camps and a larger DP association.[14]

The Harrison Report

American Jewish leaders read the letters from the soldiers and chaplains. They asked the government to send someone to study the problems in the DP camps. Earl G. Harrison went to Germany and reported back to President Harry S. Truman.

Harrison said that the army should be more considerate of the Jewish DPs and should improve their living conditions. In addition, the Jews needed permanent homes. He suggested that the United States admit more DPs and that the British open Palestine. The Harrison Report did not please Eisenhower, who knew that much more could be done to improve the lives of the DPs. But he believed that he had done a great deal in only a few months.

Help in the DP Camps

One of the improvements was the arrival of Rabbi Judah Nadich, Eisenhower's new adviser on Jewish affairs. Rabbi Nadich visited the DP camps and talked to the people. As the official adviser, Rabbi Nadich could go directly to the top generals, even to Eisenhower, with complaints. For the first time, the Jewish DPs had powerful men listening to them.[15]

The army had resisted having civilians—non-army people—working in the DP camps, probably because it could not control them. But it had no choice. The first organization to come to the camps was the United Nations Relief and Rehabilitation Administration (UNRRA). The most important Jewish groups

Jewish children attend a class about farming sponsored by the Joint at the Bergen-Belsen DP camp on August 1, 1946. The Joint and the Jewish Agency set up these programs to prepare Jewish youth for life in Palestine.

BRICHA

In 1944, former ghetto fighters and partisans in Poland began to help Jews who wanted to leave Eastern Europe. By 1945, the Jewish Brigade and other Jewish soldiers from the British army were doing the same thing in other countries. Soon, these groups connected and joined with the *Mossad L'Aliya Bet*, part of the Jewish Agency, which transported the DPs to Palestine. The branch of *Aliya Bet* moving DPs through Europe was the Bricha.[17]

The Bricha gave DPs money. It provided guides, food, and places to sleep. If people did not have birth certificates or other papers, the Bricha made fake ones. Bricha workers made up stories for border guards and the police.

The Bricha was an open secret. Some governments pretended they did not know about the Bricha because they wanted the Jews to leave their countries. The British tried to stop the Bricha in Europe and in Palestine. But they did not succeed. Between 1945 and 1948, the Bricha helped an estimated 250,000 DPs escape from Europe.[18]

were the American Jewish Joint Distribution Committee (the Joint) and the Jewish Agency for Palestine.

The Joint, a social welfare agency, paid for many refugee relief projects. The Joint brought food and clothing for the DPs. It also worked with other Jewish organizations. One of these was the Society for Trades and Agricultural Labor (ORT), which trained people for new jobs.

The Jewish Agency represented the Jewish people in Palestine. It arranged for General Eisenhower to send seven airplanes to bring teachers, other workers, and supplies from Palestine.[16] The Jewish Agency set up schools, job training centers, youth groups, and sports clubs. Many of these programs gave people new skills for life in Palestine. The Jewish Agency helped keep people's spirits up. It encouraged them to build the Jewish homeland.

The Joint and the Jewish Agency worked together. They also cooperated with others who moved Jewish survivors in and out of Germany. The name of this project was *Bricha*, which means flight or escape in Hebrew.

Important Visitors

David Ben Gurion, the head of the Jewish Agency, visited the DP camps. Then he met with General Eisenhower. They talked about improving the living conditions for the DPs. Ben Gurion spoke to the DPs at the Landsberg camp. He told them that they would be an important part of a new Jewish state. He said:

In the coming struggle you will play a decisive role. I know what you have gone through and it is not easy to make this demand of you. . . . It should not be difficult for the powers-that-be to understand why you do not wish to return to the lands of your origin. . . . [You must see yourselves] from the standpoint of the Jewish nation. At this moment—the most crucial in the past two thousand years of our history—strange as it may sound, you can accomplish a great deal. . . . From what I have seen, I know you will be strong.[19]

General Eisenhower visited Feldafing on Yom Kippur 1945. Eisenhower spoke to the crowd:

> *I am especially happy to be in a Jewish camp on the holiest day of your year. You are temporarily still here but must have patience until the day of your departure to where you want to arrive. The American Army is here to help you. I know how much you have suffered and I believe a sunny day will still come for you.*[20]

Rabbi Nadich later wrote about the importance of Eisenhower's speech to the DPs' morale:

> *His sudden unannounced visit at the Yom Kippur service at Feldafing, at which several thousand people were present, electrified the large congregation. The men and women could not believe their eyes—the great liberator himself was honoring them on the most sacred day of the Jewish year. The stormy ovation they gave him indicated the esteem, the appreciation, the love they bore for him.*[21]

Moving On

By the winter of 1945, conditions in the Jewish DP camps had slowly improved. Even so, the camps were crowded. The army did not know what to do with all the new people who arrived every day. With the help of the Bricha, the DPs from Poland, the Soviet Union, and other Eastern European countries kept coming into the camps. They were all looking for better lives, free from antisemitism and war.

The DPs in the areas under Eisenhower's command did not have an easy time. But Eisenhower did his best. He was an officer, trained to lead soldiers. He had no example or model of how to manage so many DPs.

General Eisenhower walking through the Feldafing DP camp on September 17, 1945. At Feldafing, Eisenhower spoke to the DPs on Yom Kippur.

David Ben Gurion (center with white hair) on a visit at the Landsberg DP camp.

In late 1945, a joint American and British committee—the Anglo-American Committee of Inquiry on Palestine—began to study the problem of what to do with the Jewish DPs.[22] The Jews believed Palestine was their homeland. The Arabs, who did not agree, wanted an end to the British Mandate and an Arab state without Jews.

The future of Palestine was not part of the committee's program. But it soon became the central issue. If the DPs did not have a place to go, no one could solve the problem. The committee said that the British should allow many more DPs into Palestine. They should also give up the Palestinian Mandate. Palestine should become a two-nation state with both Jewish and Arab national homes.[23]

Even with these suggestions, very little changed for nearly two years. However, the idea of dividing the land took root as a possible solution.

In November, General Eisenhower was promoted to U.S. Army Chief of Staff. General Joseph T. McNarney took over as the military governor and the commanding general in the U.S. zone in Germany. Eisenhower's tour of duty in Europe had ended. However, he did not forget the victims of the Nazi atrocity. He wrote: "Of all the distressing memories that will forever live with American veterans of the war in Europe, none will be sharper or more enduring as those of the DPs and the horror camps established by the Nazis."[24]

3 Roza Lundina

After the war, soldiers from the Allied armies were among the first to go home. Some of the Jewish soldiers in the Red Army (Soviet army), like Morris Goldman, did not want to go back to the Soviet Union. Goldman was in Berlin at the end of the war. Since he was the only survivor from his family, he decided to desert from the Red Army. He took off his uniform and put on regular clothes. He threw away his Red Army papers and became a displaced person. This was dangerous for Goldman to do. If the army had caught him, he could have been exiled or killed.[1]

Roza Lundina, also a Red Army soldier, had always planned to go home. After the Germans were driven out of her hometown, Kiev, in the Ukraine, her mother and sister had returned. They knew her brother, an army medic, was alive. Only her father was missing. The family assumed that he had died at Babi Yar in Kiev. For two days in September 1941, the Germans and the local Ukrainians murdered more than 33,000 Jews at Babi Yar. Later, tens of thousands more were killed and buried there.

Roza's War

When the war began, Roza Lundina was sixteen years old. She was very patriotic and wanted to fight for her country. But she was too young to enlist in the army. So she volunteered to defend Kiev. She said:

Soviet investigators (at left) look at a grave that was dug up at Babi Yar in Kiev, Soviet Union, in 1944. Roza Lundina believed her father was killed at Babi Yar.

> *I joined a fire-fighting brigade. We protected the roofs of the buildings from the incendiary bombs, which the Germans were dropping. We were digging anti-tank ditches on the approaches to Kiev. When the [Nazis and their local allies] were on the outskirts of Kiev in 1941, we were hastily evacuated to the Urals.*

In the Ural Mountains, east of Kiev, Lundina and her sister, Vera, helped the war effort by working on a collective farm. The soldiers and other people all over the country were hungry because they did not have enough food.

> *We collected the harvest during the late cold autumn. Vera and I would go to work half-naked. Once, while crossing a shallow*

river covered by a thin film of ice on horseback, the horse suddenly threw off the sacks filled with grain, and we had to load them up again while standing in freezing water up to our knees. Only the elderly, women, and children were left in the villages. So we all were forced to do work beyond our strength, work often fraught with danger.

Then I signed up for the construction of a metal refinery plant and was soon leading the Youth Brigade [a group of teenaged workers]. We plastered with asbestos the furnaces for the smelting of metals needed at the front. We lived in barracks with three-story bunk beds, a hundred people in each barrack.

In October 1942, as soon as she was old enough, Roza Lundina enlisted in the Red Army. Food was even scarcer than it had been on the collective farm. Her group was always hungry.

We collected leftover cabbage cores and turnips still remaining in the ground to supplement our meager rations. There were no women's clothes. They gave us trousers, puttees, boots, and pea jackets. Since I only weighed 44 kilograms [97 pounds], you

> could wrap that pea jacket around my
> body two times over.
>
> I was in a special battalion [an army
> unit, part of a regiment]. Only women were
> taught to drive. The commanders were
> men. We learned to fight, to fire guns
> and to clean them after shooting. It seems
> to me that we were treated the same as
> men soldiers.

The Road to Berlin

In April 1943, Lundina's training ended. The 35th Auto
Regiment with 2,105 people began to travel west toward the
battlefront. She drove one of the 1,166 vehicles assigned to her
group. She delivered ammunition and food and helped evacuate
the wounded.

> When our battalion stopped to rest in
> Kiev, I begged my Commander to let me
> go for two hours. I ran home. There were
> unfamiliar people living in our apartment.
> The neighbors didn't know anything about
> my father.
>
> It was difficult for the men to go
> through the war. And it was a hundred
> times more difficult for the girls.
> The Ukrainian and Polish roads had

all turned to mush during all the retreats. It was a real torment to deliver ammunition and food and drive out the wounded.

The GAZ-34 cars had long outlived their usefulness. They kept dying on us. The gasoline was really bad, and the carburetor kept clogging up. We had to clean it out with our mouths, sucking in gasoline, which often got into our stomachs.

We drove in columns of ten or twelve cars. And we always tried to help each other, but not everyone made it back after each trip. The women drivers were dying and getting wounded.

Liberation of Berlin

Roza Lundina's unit supported the soldiers in the battle for Berlin. The Germans fought from street to street and house to house. They did not want to give up their capital.

During the capture of Berlin, our regiment was delivering artillery shells to the Third Katyusha Division. On April 21, 1945, the Third Division fired the first shot on Berlin. Thus began the storming of the city, which lasted until May 2, 1945.

Roza Lundina poses with other Red Army soldiers on this statue in Berlin. Roza's unit supported the Red Army soldiers in the battle for Berlin.

After the entrance of our troops into Berlin, an organization named Hitlerjunge [Hitler Youth] took to the attics, trying to shoot at our troops and tanks with Faus bullets (special bullets that shattered the bone). But these were already the dying gasps of Nazism. Berlin fell!

I was standing on guard when the surrender was announced. At first we didn't understand. We thought we were surrounded by Germans because people were firing cannons, pistols, guns, rifles in celebration of victory. When the Company Commander came into the room and told us that this was victory, there were no bounds to our joy.

There was chaos in Berlin. The Army was trying to keep order in the towns and cities. We were helping the German people, but they were very afraid to come because they thought the soldiers will kill them. They hid themselves in the basements and in different places.

We looked for them and told them, "Nobody will touch you because you are civilians, and we want to help you." They didn't eat for many days. They had no water. The Commander of our Division told *us to tell the people that the Army kitchen will prepare some food, and we will give this food to the people, to the kids, to the old people. And one by one they came. We had a translator. We went everywhere with him. We did that June, July, two months.*

Home in Kiev

By late summer, the army began sending some of the soldiers home. On August 2, 1945, Lundina was ordered to go to the train station in Berlin. This was a very dangerous place because some Germans still had their weapons. Even though the war had ended,

Roza (center) and her group stand in front of the ruins of the Altes Museum in Berlin. It was destroyed during the war.

Roza Lundina with her husband Naum Gupper, a former Red Army soldier, who she married in 1951. Roza studied to become a teacher after the war.

they wanted to kill the Red Army soldiers. They blew up some of the trains going to the Soviet Union. But Lundina arrived home safely after two days on the train:

> I was almost 20 when I came home. I studied at a Physical Education Institute for a year. I had graduated from the eighth grade before the war. But they took me to the Institute without the [high school graduation] diploma because I had some good results in gymnastics. I told them I would pass the exams for the high school, and I did.

Lundina was an excellent gymnastics student at the institute. However, she caught malaria and had to miss her classes. After she recovered, her teachers encouraged her to return. But she decided to leave gymnastics permanently.

I enrolled at the Kiev University in 1946. When I brought in my documents to apply for admission at the Translating Department, I was rejected. I wanted to be an interpreter, but they didn't take me because I am a Jew. I knew that because on this faculty there was not one Jew, not one. Nevertheless, because of the war I had the privilege to go to this faculty. I went to the Philological Faculty and learned languages. I worked as a teacher of Russian, Literature, and English for 40 years.

At war, everyone was equal before death, but when I returned home, it was a different story. I hadn't experienced any antisemitism at the front. It all began after the war. Every year it grew harder and harder for the Jews to live in the Ukraine.

By the late '80s and early '90s, antisemitism was in full bloom. They drew swastikas [Nazi symbols] on houses. They vandalized graves and synagogues in many Ukrainian towns. Babi Yar, the site where thousands of Jews perished during the war, they wanted to level and turn into a park. The Ukrainian government remained silent about the most atrocious crime committed by humankind, the Holocaust.[2]

4 Leon Zeeberg

eon Zeeberg was born in 1918 in Lithuania. He learned
to be a tailor as a teenager. When the war started, Leon
worked in Kovno, Lithuania, about twenty miles from his
village. It was too dangerous for him to go home to his village to
be with his family. German airplanes were bombing and gangs of
men beat up Jews in the streets.

Later, Zeeberg heard that the Germans planned to put the
Kovno Jews in a ghetto. He knew that all the Jews would be
prisoners in the same neighborhood. He did not want to live
there. Despite the danger, Zeeberg decided to go home. He
wanted to be with his father, brothers, and sisters. His mother
had died the year before.

When Zeeberg arrived in his town, he saw that the Germans
had taken over. Two men with guns came to his house. They
took him to the German commandant's office. The commandant
wanted a tailor to make him a jacket.

When a new commandant came, he ordered all the Jewish
men—including Leon's brothers and father—to be killed. Only
workers who were considered useful, like Leon, were spared.
One soldier where he worked told him that Hitler planned to
kill all the Jews.

In this family portrait, Leon Zeeberg stands (center) behind his mother Esther. His sister Judith is behind their father Benyumin. They were the only members of their family to survive the war. His brothers, Meyer, Jacob, David, and Zorah, and his sister, Nechama, were murdered.

Hiding in the Forest

Leon Zeeberg convinced his friends to hide from the Germans. About ten young men went to the nearby forest with him. Many farmers knew Leon's father. One night he went to a big farm to ask for food. The farmer could not understand why Zeeberg was still alive when so many Jews were dead. He told Zeeberg:

"You can't stay here. They'll find out, and they'll shoot my family also." He was a religious Christian, and he said, "I'll save you with food." He gave us a whole sack of food with cheeses and bread and meat.

This farmer got brothers, also big farmers. He knew I am a tailor. I tell him, "Listen, nights I can come to you and make for the children clothes."

The Red Army

Although it was an open secret among some of the farmers that Zeeberg was a Jew, they did not tell the Germans. As the years passed, life became more dangerous. People began to notice that a stranger worked with the farmers. The priest sent him a message to be careful.

> Finally, in 1944, the Russians came back to Lithuania and chased the Germans. We were hiding in a bunker because of the shooting of the katyshuas, [rocket launchers carried on Army trucks] terrible, and it was a danger to stay in the houses.
>
> Then we went out, and I took from a woman a white scarf, took a stick, showed it. They came nearer, nearer.
>
> They spoke Russian. "What is your name? Who you are?" They saw already that I am not a farmer.
>
> "I am a Jew."
>
> "A Jew? How come you are here? Are you a German?"
>
> "No, I live here all the years. I am a tailor. Let me go."

The Russian soldiers put Leon Zeeberg with the Germans they had rounded up. They were looking for German soldiers, collaborators, and spies:

> Then the sergeant came over and said, "Come with me." In ten yards I see a bunker. I see a light inside. I didn't want to go there. He gave me a push. I saw a major, dark complexion, sitting by a table. On the table was a bottle of vodka.
>
> I said, "I am not a spy." Tears were dropping from my eyes. He heard my accent. "I see you are a Jew."

A Jewish partisan unit operating in the Lithuanian forests sits for a photo. Many of these partisans had been involved in resistance movements in the Kovno ghetto. Leon Zeeberg hid in the forests near Kovno to avoid capture by the Nazis.

The major told Zeeberg that the Russian army had met other people like him. He warned Zeeberg that the war was not over and that there were still Nazi soldiers in many places. After he left the bunker, Zeeberg talked to a Jewish soldier from Kiev. Then the Red Army moved on.

Zeeberg decided to go home. He wanted to find out if any of his family had survived. When he entered his village, a neighbor told him that his sister was hiding on a farm outside of town. "I came to this farm. I'll never forget it. My sister Judy, she start to cry."

Several weeks later, a Russian officer came to their house. He was looking for men to send to the Red Army. As it turned out, he was Jewish. Leon told him that he had suffered in the forest. He did not want to be a soldier. The officer said:

"No, you're not going. Enough Jewish blood was flowing in ditches. If you are going into the army, you will not come back. There will be a general attack, and a lot, a lot of people will lose their lives."

I said, "What should I do? They will be looking for me."

"I'll save you. In Kovno there is a big shop, tailoring. There work already there ten, twelve people, all Jewish tailors. The tailors are making uniforms for the Army, for the generals."

> *I said, "Yes, but how will I come to Kovno?"*
>
> *He said, "I send my soldiers three times a week to bring produce to Kovno. You have to go through borders in three places. You will have to take off your civilian clothes and put on Russian Army clothes. I'll write in my statement that I send four soldiers."*

The Long Road to the DP Camps

After the war, the Russians wanted the tailors to go back to Russia with them. But Zeeberg refused. Instead he went to Lodz, a big city in Poland. A Jewish committee in Lodz worked with the refugees. They told him to go to the DP camps in the American zone in Germany.

Some Jews, who were helping others leave Poland, gave Zeeberg money. They used back roads to smuggle the DPs over the border. This was the Bricha. Zeeberg said: "It used to take them all night. Put people in trucks. Cover them up. They wanted me to wait another day or two, but I said, 'I have to run out.' Finally, they fit me in. Like sardines we were lined up."[1]

When the DPs reached Berlin, Zeeberg felt safe for the first time. He was sent to a large DP camp called Schlachtensee. The American army provided clothing, medical treatment, and food for the DPs. Leon remembered: "There was so much food. They gave us chocolate, but the doctors told us not to eat it because we

A view of the Schlachtensee DP camp in Berlin, Germany. Leon Zeeberg went to this DP camp after leaving Lodz, Poland.

would get sick. Our bodies were not used to it, but many people did eat it and got sick."

Zeeberg lived in Schlachtensee for about six months. So many refugees poured into the camp that the Americans began to move people out. In 1946, Zeeberg was sent to Munich, Germany. While he was there, his sister Judy and her son came to live with him in the camp.

Some Americans had donated clothing to organizations like the Red Cross, which sent it to Germany for the DPs. Because the clothing seldom fit the people who received it, there was a lot of work for tailors like Leon. He said:

> They gave me a little extra room, and I stayed there. I tailored the clothes. Everybody found work. They rested. They prepared food. There was a big, big kitchen, big dining room. The main thing was soup, lots of soup.[2]

I got sick there. I got an infection in my face. Swollen and red. There wasn't doctors there in the camp. One lady said, "You have to take him to the village to the German doctor, a specialist."

He took a look. He said, "You didn't come, you would be *kaput*. You would be dead." An infection came up already on my brain. That's why I felt so terrible.

People were already leaving the camps. They go out to find friends or relatives to go to the United States.

In the camps there came Ben Gurion [the leader of the Jews in Palestine]. He yelled at us, "Don't go back to the *galut*, to the diaspora. There will be a state! Go to Israel! There'll be a state, hundred percent. . . . We must build our country for the people who survived. Go to Israel."

One morning HIAS [Hebrew Immigrant Aid Society]—it helped the immigrants—called me. "Come in the office. You have an uncle. Your father's brother knows that you survived. He wants you should come to United States."

"No, I am already going to Palestine. My mother was religious. She always taught that America is a *traife* [here meaning not

*religious] country. I don't want to go
there, but finally my uncle, my cousins
wrote a letter, got in touch with me:*

*"Laibel [his Yiddish name], we have to
see you, one survived from a big family.
You must tell us what happened. Laibel,
there's not a country. There'll be fighting
and everything." Finally, my uncle sent me
all the affidavits, the guarantees.*

An affidavit was one of the necessary documents for immigration. In it, the relatives promised that they would support the newcomer who would not ask the government for help.

So Leon Zeeberg went to the United States. He met his relatives and married Ruth Gershater, a Lithuanian immigrant from Boston. They moved to Syracuse, New York, where Leon and Ruth Zeeberg raised their family and Leon worked as a tailor.[3]

Leon Zeeberg tailored clothes donated by the Red Cross in the DP camps. This child's fur coat was worn by Mirjam Kushelewicz in the Lampertheim DP camp. She was born in the camp in 1946.

5 Dora Rytman

Dora Rytman grew up in Volozhyn, a town originally in Poland. This changed in 1939 when Germany and the Soviet Union conquered Poland and divided it between them. Volozhyn became part of the Soviet Republic of Belarus. Although the two countries promised not to fight each other, on June 22, 1941, the Germans broke the agreement and attacked the Soviet Union.

Dora was at summer camp when the war began. The camp counselors tried to calm the children. They told them that all would be well and that they would soon be going home. But within hours, the Soviet government sent a train to take the entire camp with more than five hundred campers far away from the battlefront. Dora said:

> I was absolutely terrified. I was nicknamed "the little girl who always cried." I was dying to jump out of the train, hoping that maybe I will be lucky enough to make it home. But, of course, I wasn't able to do so. I was only twelve years old.
>
> We arrived in the state of Mordovia about 300 or 400 miles east of Moscow, a very desolate place. Had I not known that

the earth was round, I was sure that this was the end of the world.

Once we came to that place, many of the children found their parents because they were running away from the Germans also. We registered in a central registration office. My parents remained under German occupation. I have never seen them again.

Evacuation

First, Dora Rytman lived at an orphanage with about 280 other children. Teenagers were sent to schools to learn to do factory work. Food was scarce, and Dora was often cold and sick. Even so, she went to school where she was an excellent student.

When Dora was thirteen, she was invited to skip high school and join a teacher-training program. Most of the other students

A group of Polish children pose for a photo at an orphanage in the Soviet Union. After Dora Rytman was evacuated from her summer camp, she lived in an orphanage in the Soviet Union.

were at least ten years older than she was. She went because she knew that the teachers would be among the first people to go home when the war ended. She wanted to find her family.

At the Belarussian Seminary, the future teachers learned teaching methods in the mornings. In the afternoons, they worked in the fields, picking potatoes, wheat, tobacco, and hemp. She also gathered flowers to make natural medicines.

Going Home

In 1944, after the Red Army pushed the Germans out of the Soviet Union, Dora and the other student teachers were sent back to Belarus. By the end of that year, Dora knew that she had to go to Volozhyn no matter how difficult the trip would be. She said:

> On December 31, 1944, I had already received letters from my hometown that no one survived. But one of the letters contained a message that if I wanted to come for a couple of days, I am welcome. It took me days and days because the entire infrastructure was broken, the roads and the trains.
>
> You had to have permits and all kinds of stuff. So I applied for my ration of bread for about four or five days. I put it in a kerchief. That was my travel food.

Dora Rytman wanted to return to her home in Volozhyn, but it was difficult to make the trip there. This photo of Dora with her daughter, Barbara, was taken later in the Schlachtensee DP camp.

Because there were no direct trains going to Dora's home, she had to change several times. Finally, she hitched a ride on a freight train carrying weapons to Germany. She sat outside on an open platform. She said:

That day was one of the biggest storms. Usually when the trains stopped, I got off and walked around so I wouldn't freeze. But this time the train stopped on an embankment which was so steep and the snow so thick that I was afraid to jump off. So I was sitting under the cannon a few miles away from my house very certain I would freeze there.

The train didn't stop at my railroad station but slowed down so I jumped off. I still had like twelve miles to walk. A young man came over to me as I was standing there early in the morning, and I was in tears, and he said, "Why are you crying?"

I said, "I've been through so much already, and I want to go to my home-town. I want to see what happened there."

He said, "I'll give you a ride." He did not have a horse and sleigh, but he was privileged to have the use of one. He went over to the peasant who was driving, and he said, "I want this young lady to be in the sleigh." He gave the man an extra few rubles.

He had two coats on. It was very cold. He gave me one of his coats, walked behind the sled. I came into my hometown this way. I jumped out, and we said good-bye.

I came to the door of the man who gave me invitation, and a little teenaged girl answers. She says, "Hey, old lady, what do you want here? Just go away from here."

I was all in rags. I said to her, "But Mr. Lavit asked me to come."

She said, "He is not home. I don't want you here. Just get out of here." I was so forlorn. When she threw me out, I had no place to go.

Dora met two young men in the street. When they recognized her, they took her to the home of her distant relative. The woman and her husband lived in a tiny room. They had little food, but what they had they shared with Dora. In exchange, she helped with the housework.

During the day, Dora wandered in the streets looking for a place to sleep that night. She went to the homes of her parents' non-Jewish friends. Her mother's best friend was not happy to see her because she had taken many of Dora's mother's things. The woman told her:

> "I know what you are looking at, but this all belongs to me because I gave food to your family in the ghetto."
>
> The ghetto was only a few months. She could not have, with all her generosity, given them so much food. I didn't even have the courage to make an issue. I walked out.

What had happened with Dora's mother's friend took place all over Poland. This theft was among the reasons why many Poles did not want the Jews to return to their homes. In addition, some Poles had moved into Jewish houses when the Germans took the Jews away.

Many Poles also believed that the Jews controlled the new Soviet-run Polish government, which they did not like. So they wanted the Jews to leave Poland.

Some people were antisemitic. Many still believed the old lie that Jews killed Christian children to make matzo (unleavened bread for the holiday of Passover). Over the centuries, Christians used the blood libel, as it is called, as an excuse to kill Jews. All of this made Poland very dangerous for the Jews. Some Jewish DPs were murdered when they returned to their hometowns.[1]

Leaving Poland

There were two types of Jews in Poland after the war. One group was made up of survivors who had been in the concentration camps, the ghettos, the forests—either hiding or fighting as partisans—or hiding in other places. The second group, like Dora, had survived in the Soviet Union and returned home.

Some in both groups believed that they would be able to rebuild their lives in Poland. But this turned out to be impossible for many people because of the antisemitism. Others were determined to leave immediately. Many in this group wanted to go to the DP camps in the American zone. They believed that the Americans would treat them better. Others preferred to go directly to Palestine, but this was very difficult. They would have to cross through many countries. And even if they reached Palestine, the British might not let them in.

No one knows exactly how many Jews left Poland right after the war. But an estimated ten thousand to thirty thousand went to Germany in the second half of 1945.[2]

Dora had to make a very difficult decision. Should she try to make a life for herself in Volozhyn or go back to the school in the Soviet Union? But something unexpected happened: "The day the war finished I met the young man again, the one who picked me up at the railroad. That day we started talking, and in a short time we decided to get married. We stayed [in Volozhyn] for about a year."

The longer Dora Rytman and her new husband, Julius, stayed in Poland, the more unwelcome they felt. Finally, in the summer of 1946, antisemitic events in another Polish town, Kielce, terrified the Jews, including the Rytmans. Dora Rytman said:

Mourners holding wreaths and banners grieve at the funeral for the victims of the Kielce pogrom. This act of violence on July 4, 1946, showed Jews that antisemitism was still strong in Poland. Dora Rytman and her family realized they needed to leave.

> The Polish people did not want the Jews back at all. So, in 1946, in the city of Kielce, they said they found the body of a little boy killed by the Jews to put blood in the matzo. And they made a pogrom, like a riot and killed about 50 of the Jews and mutilated most of the others. This was a signal saying, "Get out of here!" And so we did.

The Kielce pogrom (a brutal and violent action) was all based on a lie. A group of antisemitic men and a nine-year-old boy had made up the story. No Christian children were hurt, but many Jews were. Neither the government nor the Church told the people to stop. During the month before the pogrom, 6,647 Jews had left Poland. In the following month, about thirty thousand left. Even though the leaders were punished, the Jews knew that Poland would never be their home again.[3] Rytman said:

> We [the Jews] went by foot. We went by boat. We went by barge. We went by train. We, for instance, went by truck. We were searched at the border. We weren't allowed to have any documentation that we were from Russia because the Russians used to catch us [the Jewish DPs] and send us back.
>
> We finally came to Germany in a Displaced Persons camp where we lived for two years in Berlin. When Berlin was surrounded [in the summer of 1948], we went with the airlift. General Lucius Clay decided, instead of bringing food for the refugees, to take us out from Berlin so we wound up near Munich.

On March 4, 1949, three years after Dora and Julius Rytman left Volozhyn, they arrived in America with their baby daughter, Barbara. Rytman said:

In 1948, [the United States] had what they called the Truman Doctrine. It was so bad because [only a small number of DPs] were allowed into the United States. You had to be in perfect health. You had to have no psychological trauma. You had to have a wonderful profession. You had to sign that you would never come to depend on the government, on any social agencies, and many . . . more things. We qualified because my husband always signed himself up as a farmer. And he was a farmer at heart.[4]

Although the United States did not want to admit many Jewish DPs, Congress invited some displaced farmers to America. Dora and Julius Rytman were able to come to the United States because Julius said he was a farmer. In this photo, Julius rides his tractor on their farm in Connecticut.

6 The Lazowski Family

Ruth Rabinowitz was born in Zetel, Poland, which is now in Belarus. Ruth had an older sister and a big extended family. Ruth's father owned a lumber business, and her mother was a pharmacist. When the Soviet Union occupied the Rabinowitzes' part of Poland in 1939, the Communists took over private businesses. Ruth's father had to work for them.

For nearly two years, the Rabinowitzes lived under Soviet control until the Germans broke their treaty and invaded the Soviet Union. As the German army pushed the Red Army eastward into the Soviet Union, it took over Ruth's town and forced the Jews to move into the ghetto. She remembers saving Philip Lazowski:

> We had what is called a selection. Everyone was asked to go to the marketplace. We were waiting in line, approaching where this German was going with a finger, right, left, right, left. We saw that they were looking for people who could work for them, that had certificates. My mother had a certificate as a nurse.
>
> A little boy came over to us and said, "I'm alone here. Would you tell the German that I'm your son?"

My mother turned to him and said, "If the German will let me live with two little girls, he'll let me live with three."

He took my mother's hand on the other side. My mother was holding onto my sister. I was holding onto my sister.

At the age of ten or twelve, you were supposed to put on a Jewish star, the yellow star. His was torn in the back. My mother quickly found a pin. She knew if it would be torn off, he would be beaten by the Germans.

My father was already on the side to live. He started yelling. The German looked at my father who was a strong man and had a certificate that he could work. My mother had a certificate. So he said, "Go to the right." Philip went with us. I was seven, and he was twelve.

Maybe two weeks later, my mother went to the doctor for my sister. The doctor was on the same street where Philip lived. His mother came out to thank my mother for saving his life.

There was another selection. We ran away, and we were in the woods for over two years.

Traveling With the Bricha

In September 1944, the Red Army liberated the Rabinowitz family. But Ruth's father refused to live under a Communist government again. When he heard that Polish citizens were being allowed to return to Poland, he took the family to the city of Lublin.

In Lublin, members of the Bricha told the Rabinowitz family that they would help them travel from Poland to Italy and then on to Palestine. But they could not travel as Jews. They had to pretend to be Greek workers returning home. Ruth remembers the difficult journey through Hungary and Austria:

A Bricha guide escorts a group of Jewish DPs over the Alps into Italy. Ruth and her family traveled over the Alps into Italy after the war.

From Austria we went over the Alps at
night, walking. We got into Italy illegally.
My grandparents and parents had buried
some valuables in Zetel. There was a little
bit of jewelry and some silverware, forks
and knives. My mother wouldn't part with
it. So my father was carrying it over the
Alps, holding onto a knapsack and yelling,
"Manya, throw it away. What do you need
it for? It's too heavy to carry."

But my mother said, "No, no, no. That's
all I have left." Nobody saw us. We went at
night with a guide. All the guides were
paid off by the Bricha.

In Italy we waited to get to Palestine.
We ended up in Santa Maria d'Leuca
next to Bari. From there was Aliya Bet,
illegal immigration. But that time was
the British Mandate, and we couldn't
get in. A lot of people ended up in Cyprus
[British camps for DPs who had been
captured trying to enter Palestine
illegally]. So they would not take families
with children.

We stayed there about six months. Then
we went to Rome until 1948. In Rome we
lived in a villa.

I had no education at all until we came to Italy. There was a teacher from Palestine. Every subject was taught in Hebrew. We went to camp. In Italy my childhood came back.

My father had an aunt in the United States. But he had no idea where she lived so he put an ad in the Forward [a Jewish newspaper]. She used to read the Forward every day, and she found the ad.

Right away they contacted us and said, "Come to the United States. What are you going to do with two small children in Palestine?" At that point, we couldn't get in. So we came to the United States in July of 1948.[1]

A counselor from Palestine stands between Ruth (left) and her sister, Tanya, at a summer camp in the Italian DP camp. Ruth began receiving her education at the camp.

73

Philip Lazowski

During this same period, the boy from the ghetto, Philip Lazowski, also struggled to survive. Before the war, Philip lived in Belitzah, Lithuania, where he was the oldest of five children. His father was a fisherman, and his mother owned a fabric store.

In November 1941, the Germans ordered the Jews to leave Belitzah. The Lazowskis went to the ghetto in Zetel, where Ruth's mother saved Philip during the first roundup. During a later roundup, Philip briefly escaped. But the Nazis caught him and took him to a movie theater. He found his mother and the younger children locked up there. His brother Robert and their father were missing.

There was no way that they could all escape. Philip's mother pushed him out of a window. She said, "I want you to live, my son, may God show you the way."[2] Philip never saw any of them again.

Philip and another boy heard there were Jews in another town. Their dangerous journey to that ghetto took several days. When they arrived, Philip found his brother but not his father.

One day, their Uncle Mendel came into the ghetto. He took them out to their father in the forest. For two and a half years, they hid from the Germans and their Lithuanian allies.

In 1944, the Red Army liberated them. First, they went to Zetel where the Germans had murdered the rest of their family.

It was not a long journey, but it was a hard one, physically and spiritually. We had only the clothes we wore and a few

וועלכע ... פון דער
גאַנצע משפחה.

מיר זוכען פראַניאַ זילבערשטיין.
פון דער היים — חנה קליין, דער מאַן
— פיליפ קליין, זייערע זין — לואיס,
מיניעק און יוזשעק. זייער לעצטער
וואוינפּלאַץ איז געווען ניו יאָרק, זיי
זיינען אהין געפאָרען אין 1924. דער
 שוועסטער פון פראַניאַ קליין האָט געהייסן
חיים יאַנקעל זילבערשטיין און האָט
געוואוינט אין וואַרשע אויף נאַוויניאַר־
סקע 4. די פאַמיליע קליין האָט עמי־
גרירט פון וואַרשע. זיי וואַרען געזוכט
דורך שרה מיטעק און יענטע צעדער,
די קינדער פון מרים צעדער, פון דער
היים — זילבערשטיין. די שוועסטער
פון פראַניע קליין־זילבערשטיין.

אונזער אַדרעס:

SARA CEDER
Raw Aszej 14, Tel-Aviv, Israel

געפונען!

This advertisement was placed in a Yiddish newspaper in New York City
by Polish survivors, Sara and Irena Ceder, searching for relatives who had
immigrated to the United States before the war. Ruth's father placed such
an ad in the *Forward*, another Jewish newspaper, looking for his family in
the United States.

provisions, but we were going home. . . .
As we passed people along the way, they
looked at us in amazement, not because
of our appearance, but with an almost
incredulous belief that we were still alive.
Once in the hamlet, we saw the burned
ruins of our home just as we had left it so
many years before. . . .

The worst part of our return was the
realization that so many people who had
lived there, people who had been friends and
neighbors were dead. It was not a home-
coming because our home was nonexistent.[3]

Leaving Eastern Europe Forever

Philip's father soon realized that antisemitism had not ended with
the war. He decided they would not stay in Lithuania. Their first
stop was the city of Lodz, Poland, where they found members of
the Bricha. They wanted to go to Palestine. Philip remembers the
long journey:

We had to cross the Alps. We had to sleep
on top of the mountain because it was
snowing. The guide found some shelter
until the snow passed us by.[4]

We made our way across the country like
the prophetic wandering Jews, going from

one city to the next, using pretense where necessary to get by guards, traveling through woods and fields, always moving, always seeing that something better was ahead.

Somewhere along our journey, we boarded a train. . . . After what seemed like ages, we reached the American Zone. I saw my first American soldier. It took a while before we were permitted to enter because there was the usual showing of papers, questions to be answered, and the accompanying fear and dread that we might be turned back. Suddenly, the soldier waved us on and we were in the American Zone!

The only surviving members of the Lazowski family—Philip (left), Josef (center), and Robert—stand in the snow-covered mountains in Austria.

The DP Camp in Austria

In response to the Harrison Report, which said that the DPs had suffered enough and should not be living in terrible conditions, the American army began to improve the camps. In Austria, they took over apartment buildings and hotels for the DPs. Even so, many of the camps were crowded. Philip's family went to one of the best DP camps in Europe.[5]

From Salzburg we went to Badgastein, where my family was to remain for two years. Badgastein is one of the most beautiful places in the world with magnificent hotels and houses that seemed like vacation palaces. (Hitler used to go there for his vacations.)[6] The mountains were always capped with snow. . . .

My family and I were taken by UNRRA and placed in the Hotel Santgan, the first time in my life that I had ever been in a hotel. It was beyond belief, beyond dreams. My father, brother, and I shared a room, and we each had a bed to ourselves. It was difficult to imagine and impossible to explain what this meant to us after having lived with as many as twenty-three people in one room with hardly enough space on the floor to lie down and sleep. In addition to this untold luxury, we had food and clothing.[7]

Philip Lazowski's membership card for the Sport-Club Makkabi at the Badgastein DP camp shows that he played "fussball" (soccer) in the camp.

Philip's Reunion with the Rabinowitz Family

In 1947, the Lazowskis left Austria for the United States. Their relatives helped them settle in Brooklyn, New York.

> In 1953, while still a student, an incredible coincidence changed my life. In April, I went to a friend's wedding and at the reception, I was seated next to a young lady with whom I chatted. . . . She told me that her girlfriend's family had

saved the life of a young boy during the Nazi occupation. . . . They had lost track of the boy and didn't know his name. I could not contain myself any longer and I cried out, "I am that boy!"

The Rabinowitzes were living in Hartford, Connecticut, and I called them as soon as I could. . . . Words are inadequate to describe that reunion, for here were the people who had saved my life; people I had thought about for years, and now we had met again, under happy circumstances.[8]

During the next few years, he and Ruth Rabinowitz became good friends. Ruth studied to become a teacher. Soon, they married. Philip earned college degrees from Brooklyn College and Yeshiva University. But he always continued to study. He said, "A great dream came true for me on September 5, 1962, when I was ordained a rabbi." The Lazowskis have three sons and several grandchildren.

7 Henry Levy

Henry Levy grew up in the city of Salonica, a port on the Gulf of Salonica near the Aegean Sea.[1] In the early years, the ancient Greeks controlled the city. Then it became part of three empires, one after the other: the Roman Empire, the Byzantine Empire, and the Ottoman Empire. In 1912, the Greek army captured Salonica from the Ottomans.

Jews have lived in Salonica for more than two thousand years. Over the centuries, Jewish refugees from many countries settled there. Each group built its own community.

The largest group of refugees came from Spain and Portugal to escape the Spanish Inquisition in 1492. They were called Sephardim from the word Sepharad, their name for Spain. Among them were Henry Levy's ancestors. The Sephardim had borrowed many Spanish customs. They had their own way of practicing the Jewish religion. They cooked different foods. They spoke a Spanish-Jewish language, called Ladino Español. The Sephardic traditions became the way of life in Salonica.

On April 6, 1941, the German army invaded Greece. It captured Salonica on April 9. During the next few weeks, the Germans and their allies forced some Jews out of their homes and businesses. They stole or destroyed religious objects, art, and books. Even so, for about a year, Jewish life went on. Then things changed.[2]

The Levy family lived in Salonica, Greece, for many generations. In this photo taken in February 1940, from left to right, Henry's mother, Esther; his brother Jack Vital; Henry; and his father, Joseph. His oldest brother Edgard is not pictured.

Henry Levy's Unsuccessful Escape

Teenager Henry Levy stayed with his family in Salonica for almost a year after the Germans captured his city. In March 1942, his parents finally agreed that he should try to escape to Palestine. He went with three friends. Only Benjamin Saltiel and Henry Levy were Jewish. Levy wrote in his memoirs: "All gates were closed tight for us the Jews to run away to the free world. The British White Paper prohibited us to enter legally to Palestine. The only option was to escape and to enter illegally."

Less than two weeks later, Levy and Saltiel were arrested near the Turkish border. A friend of one of

In September 1943, the Germans ordered the chief rabbi of Athens, Elias Barzilai, to make a list of all the Jews and the people who helped them. The rabbi called upon the archbishop of the Greek Orthodox Church for help.

Archbishop Damaskinos announced that the Church did not approve of the Nazis' actions. He told the Jews to leave Greece and asked the Greeks to help them. He arranged for many Jews to receive false baptism certificates. He worked with the Athens chief of police to give thousands of Jews new identity papers. Documents like these saved many lives.

Then Archbishop Damaskinos did something that no other national church leader in Europe had done. With the help of a poet, Angelos Sikelianos, he wrote a protest letter. Many leaders of Greek organizations signed the letter. It began:

> The Greek People were rightfully surprised and deeply grieved to learn that the German Occupation Authorities have already started to put into effect a program of gradual deportation of the Greek Jewish community of Salonika. . . .
>
> According to the terms of the armistice, all Greek citizens, without distinction of race or religion, were to be treated equally by the Occupation Authorities. The Greek Jews . . . [are] law-abiding citizens who fully understand their duties as Greeks.[3]

A German officer leads three Jewish men in forced exercises on Freedom Square in Salonica, Greece. On July 11, 1942, about ten thousand men were forced to do exercises under brutal conditions. After Germany invaded Greece, the Nazis began placing many restrictions on Jews.

the non-Jews had reported them to the Germans. The Germans moved the boys from prison to prison, and they eventually ended up in the Salonica ghetto.

By 1943, the Jewish community in Salonica was destroyed. The Germans forced the Jews to wear Stars of David. They forced them into ghettos. Between March and July, they deported more than 45,000 Jews.[4] Henry Levy lost his parents, Joseph and Esther; his brother Edgard; and his sister-in-law Margot in Auschwitz-Birkenau.

Auschwitz-Birkenau

Henry Levy and Benjamin Saltiel were taken to the Salonica train station and put on a train to Poland. They thought they were going to the Krakow ghetto. But they were going to the biggest Nazi camp, Auschwitz, near the Polish city of Oświęcim (Auschwitz in German). Different parts of Auschwitz had certain purposes. Auschwitz-Birkenau was the main killing center for the Jews. Other sub-camps housed forced laborers.

By the end of the war, an estimated 1.1 million Jews, 74,000 Poles, 21,000 Roma, 15,000 Soviet prisoners of war, and 10,000–15,000 people from other countries had been murdered in the Auschwitz complex of camps.[5] Levy wrote:

> I saw a long line of cars ordinarily used for the transport of cattle. Now, behind securely locked doors, they were jam-packed with human cargo—fellow Jews.
>
> Before being tossed in like so much baggage by an SS trooper, a Red Cross volunteer managed to hand me a small cloth packet. Its contents included a pair of underwear, two pairs of socks, toothpaste and toothbrush, two loaves of bread, a few cans of sardines, a hunk of cheese, salami, and soap.
>
> There was barely room for my bruised and aching body in this boxcar full of

some eighty whimpering and screaming people of all ages.

Our terrible journey ended after ten days. Those of us who survived, stumbled out of the cars to be greeted by the shouts and jabs of gun slinging "monsters" urging us to hurry.

We were ordered to undress. The barbers were waiting. Still a teenager, I was no longer to be known by my given name but rather the number 120928 tattooed on my arm. I was hurled into a dark world of death and destruction.

In Auschwitz-Birkenau, the Jews of Greece came face-to-face for the first time with the Jews from Eastern and Western Europe. We found that we had little in common with them. With our olive complexions and darker hair, we were even different in appearance. They spoke Yiddish [the language of the Eastern European Jews], Polish, German. Some spoke Hebrew. We spoke Ladino Español, Greek, French, Italian. Even our Hebrew was different. Because we were strangers to them, they refused to accept us as truly Jews.

A large group of Jews from Hungary is taken off cattle cars at the unloading ramp at Auschwitz-Birkenau. Henry Levy suffered through the same terrible journey aboard the trains before arriving at Auschwitz.

The Warsaw Ghetto

The Warsaw ghetto in Poland had over 400,000 Jews jammed together inside its walls making it the largest ghetto established by the Nazis. In 1942, the Germans began to transport Jews from the Warsaw ghetto to Treblinka, a death camp. At least 265,000 Jews from Warsaw were murdered at Treblinka. When some people in the ghetto learned the truth, they decided to resist. If they were going to die, they would go down fighting.

The first big test for the Jewish resistance group, called the ZOB (Polish initials for Jewish Combat Organization), came on January 18, 1943. When the Nazis began to round up the Jews, the ZOB fought back and saved some people.

On April 19, 1943, the Nazis moved into the ghetto again. The ZOB was ready. But, they were overmatched by the Germans. Those who could not fight hid in shelters, known as bunkers.

At first, the Jewish resistance was successful, but the Nazis sent in thousands of men with many weapons. For nearly a month, the Nazis blew up and burned the ghetto, killing about seven thousand Jews. They sent most of the survivors to Nazi camps, primarily to Treblinka.

On May 16, 1943, the uprising was over. The Nazis set up a concentration camp on the site of the Warsaw ghetto and brought in forced laborers, including Henry Levy, to tear down the remaining buildings and clean up the rubble.[6] Levy wrote:

Our first assignment was to remove the bodies of the SS officers and men who had died fighting in the Jewish resistance of the Warsaw Ghetto. The brave Jews died fighting this superior strength with only their bare hands as weapons. The Jewish resistance fought as real heroes.

We Greek Jews stuck together like brothers. We did not steal from one another but were there to help one another in every way. Though the Eastern European Jews had no desire to befriend us, they did respect us for our devotion to our own and our ability to maintain our dignity as Jews and human beings under these terrible conditions.

THE *SONDERKOMMANDO* REVOLTS AT AUSCHWITZ-BIRKENAU

Henry saw the Nazis murder huge numbers of people in Auschwitz-Birkenau. He knew the members of the *Sonderkommando* were the prisoners forced to collect the victims' possessions and clean the gas chambers and crematoria. Although Henry was in Warsaw during the Sonderkommando revolts, he learned about them later. The first took place in September 1944 when about two hundred Sephardic Jews decided to fight back.[7] Henry wrote:

> *There were some who were courageous and risked their lives to prevent the killing of the Hungarian Jews. [Men from Salonica and Athens] organized a revolt against the Germans. Rallying a group of 135 Greek Jews and some Sephardic Jews from France, they managed to blow up and destroy Crematoria #3.*
>
> *My brother Edgard was hanged by the Germans for helping to blow up the crematoria. It gives me satisfaction to know that his life was not lost in vain. All my compatriots sacrificed their lives to save others.*

Polish Jews led the second revolt. On October 7, they attacked the guards and set fire to Crematorium IV and the adjacent gas chamber. This attack failed also, and 451 members of the Sonderkommando were killed, as were some of the women who had stolen the explosives.[8]

A group of Jews stand facing a wall with their hands up after being captured by Nazi soldiers during the Warsaw ghetto uprising. Henry Levy was forced to remove the dead bodies and clear the ruins in Warsaw after the uprising.

The Long Road to Freedom

Henry Levy's group had been in Poland for more than a year when they heard that the Soviet Red Army was approaching. In November 1944, their captors—mostly Poles, Lithuanians, and Ukrainian SS men—marched them out of the camp. The prisoners did not have food, water, or enough clothing. Their guards were cruel and abusive, torturing and killing many Jews as they walked to Germany.

> *We began to talk of revolt. Weak from exposure and hunger and with no weapons, we knew any such attempt would prove futile. Though we outnumbered them, we could not murder our captors or prevent them from murdering us. At night we were chained leaving no hope for escape.*

Dachau

In 1933, the Nazis opened their first major concentration camp, Dachau in southern Germany, for political prisoners. Later, other groups were imprisoned there as well. In the early years, Jews were not sent to Dachau unless they belonged to another so-called "anti-Nazi" group, such as the Communist Party. Dachau became a training school for SS guards and a center for medical experiments on living people. By 1944, many of the prisoners at Dachau were forced laborers working in war industries.

Levy believes that only 985 of the 1,481 prisoners survived the twenty-seven-day march to reach Dachau.

Finally, we arrived in Dachau. The German General Commandant of Dachau was shocked at our physical condition. He immediately opened an investigation. Dachau for us was heaven. But our stay there was to last only for a week. He had orders from Berlin. As Jews, we did not belong in Dachau.

[At the next camp] machine guns pointed at us. The guards screamed that they would kill us like dogs if we did not move faster. They ordered us to undress. We hesitated. At that moment the Allied air force began bombing the surroundings of the camp.

I was working in a cement factory for the manufacture of concrete blocks with steel wire. We made sure that 40% of those produced were defective. My friends, Daniel and David, worked in an ammunition factory. They succeeded in producing defective bullets meant for machine guns.

Liberation

As the Allied armies drove into Germany, the Nazis took many prisoners out of the camps. They forced some to walk and others to ride on crowded freight trains. No one knew where they were going or why. Beginning on March 27, 1945, Levy's group rode around the country for thirty-three days. They often changed direction because Allied planes were bombing the train tracks. Some of the trains carrying the prisoners were hit.

> *We awoke one morning to find the doors of the freight cars unlocked. There were no guards in sight, only uniforms, guns and boots strewn all over the ground. Now, we knew the war was over. We disembarked, screaming with joy. The date was May 1, 1945. We were liberated outside of Munich by the Third U.S. Army under General Patton. We were taken by U.S. Army trucks to Feldafing.*

These boots were worn by a female prisoner, Ala Brand, at Auschwitz and on a "death march." Henry Levy was forced on such a march by his captors when the Red Army was closing in on German positions in Poland.

After the War

Henry Levy organized a business in the Feldafing DP camp. He got cigarettes from UNRRA and the Red Cross and sold them to the Germans. This was called the black market. After three months, Levy went to Italy with the Bricha. From there, he planned to go to Salonica to look for his brother Jack. He did not know that Jack had been murdered.

Levy lived in Italy for eight months until the Greek Embassy in Rome gave him the papers he needed to go home. When he arrived, he found that 94 percent of the Salonica Jewish community was gone. Only 1,200 Sephardic Greeks returned to their city.[9]

Levy still had some of the money he had earned in Feldafing selling cigarettes. He opened a small shop. He met Ida Levy, a survivor from Vienna, Austria. Ida had been in Bergen-Belsen with her parents. Soon, they married.[10]

This photo of Henry Levy was taken in Munich, Germany, on June 6, 1945. The uniform he is wearing was altered by a tailor because he weighed less than 80 pounds. He paid for the alterations with two packs of cigarettes, which were used as currency in the black market.

In April 1947, Levy was drafted into the Greek army. He served in the army until December 1950. Because the Greeks were fighting the Communists, the United States welcomed Henry Levy as a freedom fighter. He did not have any trouble getting permission for his family to come to America.[11]

8   Bernard Ostfeld

Bernard Ostfeld grew up in Germany with two older brothers, David and Leo, and a younger brother, William. Bernard was a ballet dancer and pianist. His father owned several shoe stores. The Ostfeld family had a comfortable life.

In 1932, when the Nazi Party came to power, it did not allow David to work as a doctor. Nazi boys beat up William for dating a non-Jewish girl. The family decided that the brothers should leave Germany. Through a friend of his father, Bernard got a job dancing in Italy.

In order to leave Germany, Bernard Ostfeld needed a passport. This government document allowed citizens to go from one country to another. He also needed permission to enter Italy:

> An employee from the government said, "We're very sorry. We cannot give you a passport because you are Jewish. But we will give you a passport apolide, a passport without a country."
>
> When I went to the Italian Consulate, they said, "What piece of paper is this?" I said, "This is an apolide passport or Nansen passport." Nansen was a Norwegian man who created the Nansen passport for people without country.

Ostfeld pretended to have a stomach ulcer. He said he needed to go to a warm climate for his health. The Italians let him in.

Life in Italy

Ostfeld became a successful dancer in Italy. He worked with famous dancers, and his troupe danced for the king of Monaco. But Italy began to change its attitude toward Jews. Benito Mussolini, the dictator of Italy, and Hitler became allies in 1936. At first, Mussolini did not bother the Jews. But Hitler wanted him to make anti-Jewish laws.

Bernard Ostfeld (right) stands with his brother William in this photo taken before he left Germany in 1933.

Italian Jews were forced to work for the government. Some shoveled sand or cut logs. By the late 1930s, Ostfeld was not allowed to dance with his company. His friends paid him secretly to teach dancing or to play the piano. Even so, he said, "The Italians were human. They arrested only if necessary."

Meanwhile, Ostfeld had been trying to get permission to go to the United States. Anyone who wanted to settle in the United States had to have an invitation and other documents from a relative who was already a citizen. "In 1937, the American

Consulate in Rome called me. 'You have an affidavit from your aunt in New York. But you have to wait in line because only 39,000 Germans can leave Germany.'"

Ostfeld was stuck in Italy. However, Jews from other parts of Europe continued to see Italy as a refuge. They hoped that the Italians would not hurt them. Some thought that they would find boats to take them to Palestine.

Prisoners

Mussolini declared war on June 10, 1940. Under pressure from the Germans, the Italians began to round up the Jews. They planned to send them to special camps.

> *Two men came to my apartment and said, "Bernard Ostfeld, you have to come to the police department."*
>
> *They put me on a chain. They took me to the police department where I stayed all day long. There came a paddy wagon, and they brought me to Regina Coeli. This was the jail where they put all the Jewish foreign people. I saw several of my friends.*

The camps were not ready. So the Italians kept Bernard's group in the jail for about a month. Then they loaded them onto a train. They took them to a concentration camp in Calabria in southern Italy. They were chained together in groups of five, eighty people altogether.

Children sit around a table in the Ferramonti concentration camp in Calabria, Italy. Bernard Ostfeld was interned at this camp during the German occupation of Italy.

No one wanted to be in these camps, but they were not like the camps in other parts of Europe. Families stayed together, and the children went to school.[1]

The Jews did not have enough to eat, but they were treated relatively well. Ostfeld saw someone punished harshly only once when a man tried to run away. Ostfeld and his brother knew that there was nowhere for them to go even if they did manage to escape. He said:

> *When I was in the concentration camp, I got another letter from the American Consulate in Naples. "We are happy to announce that your affidavit will come through. You can go to America in '42." I was so furious I took my letter and destroyed it. How can they have the nerve to send to somebody in concentration camp a letter and tell them to wait another year to go to America?*

Ostfeld's camp was located in a very swampy region. The mosquitoes there infected many prisoners with malaria. People died from the disease. Ostfeld took two quinine pills a day to protect himself from getting the disease.

When one of the men in his bunk caught malaria, Ostfeld panicked. He took ten pills at once. This made him very ill. The camp officials took him to a doctor in town. They arranged for him to stay in the home of a Nazi sympathizer. He was closely guarded in the man's shoe store. Ostfeld convinced the camp director to allow his brother to join him.

Ostfeld and the doctors did not know at that time that quinine caused deafness. Ostfeld recovered, but he lost most of his hearing.[2]

Surrender

On July 25, 1943, a group of powerful Italians forced Mussolini out of office and arrested him. King Victor Emmanuel III and

While in Rome, Italy, Bernard Ostfeld used a forged French passport for five months to work in a school of priests. This collage of forged French identification papers and rubber stamps is on display at the United States Holocaust Memorial Museum in Washington, D.C.

General Pietro Badoglio led the new government. They wanted to end the war.

On September 8, 1943, the Italians surrendered to the Allies. But their partners, the Germans, did not give up so easily. The Allies had to push them north toward Germany. This took more than another year of fierce fighting.

Meanwhile, that summer, American soldiers closed the concentration camps in Calabria. Bernard and William had to be very careful. Even though they were free, there were still Nazis and antisemitic Italians who would kill them if they could. First, the brothers hid in the mountains of southern Italy. Then they went to Rome, which remained under German control.

In many places, Christians helped them. One group gave Bernard Ostfeld a false passport with a French name. For about five months, he lived in a college for French priests. He translated letters for the people living there. He remained safe because the Germans could not go into the Vatican. However, Ostfeld was afraid that the Germans would break in and find them.

Liberation in Rome

Bernard Ostfeld had some money because he taught German and French. His friends at the opera where he had worked also collected money for him. The brothers rented a small apartment. They were at home on June 4, 1944, when they heard a lot of noise and shouting in the streets:

I took my brother—we lived near Piazza de Espana by the steps there—and we ran out. We heard already on the loudspeaker, "We are coming from America. We are friends of yours," in Italian and in English.

When we saw the first soldier, we embraced and kissed him. We went arm in arm with them. Then we heard shooting. We saw shooting from the roofs, and I said to my brother, "You want to get killed at the last moment." We went to our place and went to bed. And that is the first night I slept.

The next morning at 7 o'clock, we went to the most famous newspaper. It was one sheet: "Americans Occupy Rome!"

A jeep came by. They said, "Who speaks English?"

I said, "You can talk with me. I speak English."

"You speak such good English. Where did you learn English?"

I said, "In Germany, in high school."

"What you doing here?"

I said, "I am a German Jew."

They started to embrace us. They were both reporters from Brooklyn, both Jewish.

> They said, "Did you have breakfast?
> Come with us."
>
> We came in a hall, all officers. We
> are sitting there in rags, and there came
> the waiter. The first time I saw scrambled
> eggs and white bread, and everything
> what you just wanted. I looked to my
> brother, and I said, "This is so fantastic.
> I feel like a king." It was the first breakfast
> in years.

That same day, the Jewish reporters had to leave Rome. The war had not ended, and they had to go north with their army unit.

Working for Food

After a short time, Bernard Ostfeld found a job with the American United Service Organization (USO). The USO put on shows for the American soldiers. "We got money. We got a loaf of bread because everybody was starving and a piece of soap. We got a can of milk. We got this for every show we gave. I was so weak. I was thirty pounds underweight when the war was finished."

Ostfeld played the piano at a rest camp for American soldiers. He put the food they gave him into his pockets and took it home for his brother. Several months later, the opera called him, and he started to rehearse for shows. By now it was 1946. Ostfeld played piano in the morning and worked at a Hebrew Immigrant Aid Society (HIAS) distribution center in the afternoon. Ostfeld said:

Large crowds attend a ceremony in Rome after the city was liberated on June 4, 1944. The day Rome was liberated, Bernard and William Ostfeld had their "first breakfast in years."

> *I could work there because they wanted people from the camps. We were in the warehouse. We put the things in cartons. Everybody got canned food, sugared milk, flour. We got some extra packages to take home if the food wasn't in good shape, maybe smashed or something.*

SS *Marine Perch*

Ostfeld wanted to go to the United States, but he did not have the right papers. He had lost his chance to go in 1942. In 1947, something completely unexpected happened:

Bernard Ostfeld appears in two photos in a newspaper article written after the war. He eventually emigrated to the United States.

Bernard Ostfeld (left) as he looked in 1939, while on tour in Tripoli with a ballet company. At right, in a photo taken in Rome in 1945, after four and a half years in a Fascist concentration camp, he has lost 30 pounds and most of his hearing.

Memories of a 'Lucky' Jew

I had a ballet student who worked with HIAS. She said, "I will give you a chance to go to America. You can take a ship from Naples. You get the trip paid because you have no money." She arranged through her friendship with the director. There came my brother too.

When we came to Naples, a man came to me and said, "Somebody wrote already from Rome about you. I have here sixty girls and boys. They are orphans coming from Poland. I want that you are the captain of this group."

I said, "I will be delighted to take them." They were fifteen/sixteen years old. HIAS found out they were with Christian foster parents. The Jewish people had abandoned them because they knew that the Nazis would take them and kill them as they had killed so many people.

The SS Marine Perch was an American liberty ship, a military ship. There were 2,000 people on a ship built for 1,000. A man who took care of the food said, "You always speak Yiddish with these children. Who are they?"

I said, "They are orphans from Jewish people."

He said, "Shalom, I am Jewish too." He ran out to his two bakers, and they brought Italian ice cream in slices every day. It was the friendship he wanted to give them.

I arrived in America. Everybody was seeing the Statue of Liberty. When we came there, it was raining. Everybody cried. We were free! We were free! It was our new home country.[3]

CONCLUSION

After the war, millions of non-Jewish displaced persons went home, but an estimated one million remained. Many non-Jews who stayed did so for political reasons. Large numbers of these DPs were farmers or had job skills that other countries needed. For example, in 1946, Belgium invited twenty thousand coal miners and their families to settle there.[1] Non-Jewish workers were more welcome than Jews in many countries. There was still no solution for the Jews. Some wanted to live near their relatives wherever they were. Others wanted to go to Palestine. They worried constantly about where and how they would make new lives.

Lottie, Jacob, and Arie Rothenberg were DPs from Koretz, a city in Poland first occupied by the Russians and then by the Germans. Lottie and their young son, Arie, had been in hiding throughout the war. Jacob had fought with the partisans. For several years, they lived in Camp Herzog, a DP camp near the city of Kassel, Germany. Lottie Rothenberg remembered:

> Camp Herzog held about 400 people. It seemed that no one was in a hurry to come to our rescue. We lived in temporary homes in the camp where we shared a room with one or two other families. We slept on canvas

> cots along the walls and ate our meals
> on a long, bare table. Except for two long
> benches, those were all the furnishings.
>
> Our children, the most miraculous
> survivors, needed a regular school and a
> normal life, which the camp was unable to
> provide. Most of all, we needed encourage-
> ment to restore our faith in humanity. We
> worried about visas, quotas, and medical
> problems, which stood in our way before we
> could join the civilized world once more.[2]

Lottie Rothenberg and the other DPs in the camps did not know that the larger political situation around them was changing.

American Immigration Laws

Groups like the Citizens Committee on Displaced Persons pressured Congress to allow more DPs to enter the United States. But every country had a quota of how many people could enter the United States each year. The countries with the most Jewish DPs had very low quotas. Even so, about forty thousand DPs of all sorts arrived in America in 1945 and 1946.[3]

In 1948, Congress passed the Displaced Persons Act, but it had so many rules that it kept out many Jewish DPs. Although President Harry S. Truman signed the law, he was not happy with it. He said, "In its present form this bill is flagrantly discriminatory. It mocks the American tradition of fair play."[4]

By the time the act ended in 1950, 43,150 DPs had moved to the United States.[5] When Congress finally amended the DP Act to bring in more people, this helped the Jews. This raised the admission total to four hundred thousand people.[6] By 1952, another five thousand DPs had settled in the United States.[7]

The British Mandate for Palestine

The British continued to bar most of the Jewish DPs from entering Palestine. They did not want to anger their Arab friends. In 1946, the British set up camps on the island of Cyprus to house the Jewish DPs the Bricha tried to bring into Palestine. In contrast, at about the same time, the British invited more than one hundred thousand DP workers to England.[8] Few were Jewish.

The situation in Palestine was growing worse. The Jews and the Arabs each believed their history entitled them to the land.

Jewish DPs participate in a protest against Britain's immigration policy to Palestine at the Neu Freimann Displaced Persons camp in Munich, Germany.

There were riots and murders. The Jews and the Arabs fought each other. So did the Jews and the British.

Finally, in February 1947, Ernest Bevin, the British foreign secretary, turned the Palestinian Mandate over to the United Nations (UN). The UN set up the United Nations Special Committee on Palestine (UNSCOP) to study the problem and make suggestions. The UN General Assembly would vote on what to do.

UNSCOP talked to the Jewish DPs in the European camps. It went to Palestine to look at the community built by the Jews. The Arabs refused to take part in the discussions. They believed that Palestine should be an Arab country, and they were not interested in compromising.

Exodus 1947

Jewish leaders decided to show UNSCOP and the world that they were determined to bring the DPs to Palestine. On July 11, 1947, the *Exodus 1947* sailed from France with 4,515 Jewish DPs on board. The British attacked the unarmed ship, injuring thirty people and killing one American sailor. As soon as the *Exodus* docked in Haifa, the British forced the DPs to board British ships to go back to France. Although it was hot and uncomfortable, most of the DPs would not leave the ships in France. They refused to eat. DPs in the camps held sympathetic hunger strikes.

On August 22, the British ships sailed for Germany. Again, the DPs refused to cooperate. The British used fire hoses and sticks to force the people to leave the ships and return to the DP camps.

The *Exodus 1947* coming to port in the Haifa, Palestine, harbor. The British forced the thousands of Jewish DPs onboard the *Exodus* to board British ships and go back to France.

More than eight thousand DPs in Germany held a protest. All over the world people heard about the *Exodus* and the DPs who had no home. The international protests embarrassed the British. Meanwhile, the Bricha had started to take the *Exodus* passengers out of the camps again and transport them to Palestine.[9]

Israel

On August 31, 1947, UNSCOP announced that the mandate should end. Three months later, on November 29, the UN General Assembly voted to divide Palestine into Arab and Jewish countries. Everyone knew the war would begin as soon as the British left the country. The *Hagana*, the unofficial Jewish army, recruited volunteers from the DP camps. They would be soldiers

This identification card issued to three-year-old Mendel Goldband stated that he was passenger no. 633 on the *Exodus*. Thousands of DPs in Germany held a protest march after learning about the horrible treatment the *Exodus* passengers received.

for the new nation. It also called for Jewish soldiers from other countries to help.[10]

On May 14, 1948—the day after the mandate ended—David Ben Gurion, the first prime minister, declared the State of Israel. Israel immediately repealed the British White Paper of 1939. This opened the new country to the Jewish DPs. Lottie Rothenberg celebrated the birth of Israel with her friends and family in Camp Herzog:

112

"Mazel tov! [Congratulations!]" cried the male voice over the loudspeaker in the center of the camp. "We have a home at last, a land. Palestine is ours."

It took a long while for the message to sink in—that Israel had been proclaimed a state. Somehow it sounded too unrealistic for something so good to happen. After all those years of misery, plight, and tragedy, how could it be? It was wet and muddy as we formed a circle within a circle and began to dance. How we danced!

On May 14, 1948, David Ben Gurion declared the State of Israel. In this photo taken in 1948, Jewish DPs on board a train wave good-bye to people as they leave Munich, Germany, headed to France en route to Israel.

Between May 15 and the end of 1948, 25,526 DPs left Europe for Israel.[11] Other DPs traveled from the British detention camps on Cyprus. More than half of the DPs went to Israel and the rest to the United States and other countries.

Only a small number of those who could not or would not leave Europe remained. By the end of 1951, all the camps but Foehrenwald near Munich had closed. Germany took over this last camp and cared for the final DPs. Many of these were old or ill. Some had gone to Israel, but unhappy with the life there, had returned. Others were too upset by the war to move anywhere. The Germans closed Foehrenwald in 1957.[12] At last, all of the DPs had found new homes. Rothenberg said:

> For the first time after so many years, we could sing again. Our voices rang loud and clear across the land of the murderers who destroyed the lives of millions of people. Tucked away as we were, in a small corner of Germany, we wished that the whole world could hear us and understand that our nation was not wiped out yet. We were very much alive.[13]

1932
July 31—The Nazis win the German national elections. Bernard Ostfeld leaves Germany for Italy.

1933
January 30—Adolf Hitler becomes chancellor of Germany.

1934
August 2—President Paul von Hindenberg dies, and Hitler takes over Germany.

1936
October 25—Germany and Italy become allies.

1939
August 24—Germany and the Soviet Union sign a pact not to go to war.

September 1—Germany invades Poland.

1940
Bernard Ostfeld is arrested and sent to an Italian concentration camp.

1941
June 22—The Germans break their friendship pact and invade the Soviet Union.

June 25—Leon Zeeberg is caught up in the first anti-Jewish riot in Kovno, Lithuania.

November—Philip Lazowski's family is forced to leave their home and go into a ghetto.

December 7—The Japanese bomb Pearl Harbor, and the United States declares war on Japan.

December 11—The United States declares war on Germany.

1942

March—Henry Levy leaves Salonica, Greece, and tries unsuccessfully to flee to Palestine.

November—Dwight D. Eisenhower becomes the supreme commander of the Allied expeditionary forces in Europe.

1943

May 16—The Nazis defeat the Jewish fighters in the Warsaw ghetto uprising.

August—The Nazis send Henry Levy from Auschwitz to Warsaw to clean up the ghetto.

September 29—The Nazis take the Zukerman family to Westerbork.

1944

The Bricha begins to take displaced persons (DPs) out of Poland.

June 4—The Allies liberate Bernard Ostfeld in Rome.

Summer—The Red Army, passing through Lithuania, liberates Leon Zeeberg.

September—The Red Army liberates Ruth Rabinowitz Lazowski.

December 31—Dora Rytman sets out alone for her hometown, Volozhyn.

1945

April 12—General Eisenhower visits the Ohrdruf concentration camp.

April 23—The Red Army liberates the Zukerman family in Bergen-Belsen.

April 30—Hitler commits suicide.

May 1—The American army liberates Henry Levy from a train in Germany.

May 7—German General Alfred Jodl surrenders to Eisenhower.

July 14—The Zukerman family returns to Holland on an American hospital train.

August 2—Roza Lundina completes her army service and returns to the Soviet Union.

1946

July 4—The Kielce pogrom frightens thousands of Jews into leaving Poland.

1947

February—The British turn the Palestinian Mandate over to the United Nations (UN).

July 11—The ship *Exodus* sets out for Palestine with more than four thousand illegal DPs aboard.

August 22—The British send the *Exodus* passengers back to DP camps in Germany.

November 29—The UN votes to divide Palestine into two countries.

1948

May 14—David Ben Gurion declares the new Jewish State of Israel.

June 24—The United States passes a very limited Displaced Persons Act.

1949

March 4—Dora, Julius, and Barbara Rytman arrive in the United States.

1953

Philip Lazowski is reunited with Ruth Rabinowitz and her family.

1957

Foehrenwald, the final DP camp, closes.

Introduction

1. Henry Levy, *The Jews of Salonica and the Holocaust: A Personal Memoir* (Unpublished manuscript, the Jewish Historical Society of Greater Hartford, 1991), p. 1.
2. Hayim-Meir Gottlieb in Leo W. Schwartz, ed., *The Root and the Bough* (New York: Rinehart & Company, 1949), pp. 309–310. This quotation comes from a multi-language group diary of young survivors of Buchenwald. After the war, they founded Kibbutz Buchenwald, a community and training program for those wanting to form a kibbutz in Palestine. Novelist Meyer Levin translated many of the entries and arranged for the translation of others.
3. Lester Eckman and Chaim Lazar, *The Jewish Resistance: The History of the Jewish Partisans in Lithuania and White Russia During the Nazi Occupation 1940–1945* (New York: Shengold Publishers, 1977).

Chapter 1.   The Zukerman Family

1. Personal interview with John Faitella, June 26, 2007.
2. Yehuda Bauer, *Out of the Ashes: The Impact of American Jews on Post-Holocaust European Jewry* (Oxford: Pergamon Press, 1989), p. 36.
3. Personal interview with Debora Zukerman Fish, February 11, 2008.
4. Adi Zukerman wrote his letter in German. It was translated into English by an unknown translator and is on file at the Jewish Historical Society of Greater Hartford. This is an edited version of the letter.

Chapter 2.   Dwight D. Eisenhower

1. Dwight D. Eisenhower, *Crusade in Europe* (Garden City, N.Y.: Doubleday, 1948), pp. 408–409.
2. Ibid., p. 74
3. Ibid., p. 428.

4. Ibid., p. 188.

5. Judah Nadich, *Eisenhower and the Jews* (New York: Twayne Publishers, 1953).

6. Abraham S. Hyman, *The Undefeated* (Hewlett, N.Y.: Gefen Publishing House, 1993), p. 59.

7. Eisenhower, pp. 439–440.

8. Alex Grobman, *Rekindling the Flame: American Jewish Chaplains and the Survivors of European Jewry, 1944–1948* (Detroit: Wayne State Press, 1993), p. 41.

9. Hyman, p. 146.

10. Personal interview with Beatrice Faymann Brodie, January 10, 2008.

11. Yehuda Bauer, *Flight and Rescue: Brichah: The Organized Escape of the Jewish Survivors of Eastern Europe, 1944–1948* (New York: Random House, 1970), pp. 54, 62–67, 96–97.

12. Yehuda Bauer, *Out of the Ashes: The Impact of American Jews on Post-Holocaust European Jewry* (Oxford: Pergamon Press, 1989), p. 44.

13. Ibid., pp. 47–48.

14. Grobman, pp. 106–109.

15. Hyman, pp. 33–44.

16. Ibid., p. 389.

17. Ephriam Dekel, *B'RICHA: Flight to the Homeland* (New York: Herzl Press, 1973), pp. 8–11.

18. Hyman, pp. 198–204.

19. Leo W. Schwartz, *The Redeemers: A Saga of the Years 1945–1952* (New York: Farrar, Straus and Young, 1953), p. 51.

20. Quoted in Hyman, p. 63 from the DP newspaper, *Unzer Weg* (Our Way).

21. Nadich, pp. 129–130.

22. Hyman, pp. 87–100.

23. Ibid., pp. 117–133.

24. Eisenhower, p. 441.

Chapter 3. Roza Lundina

1. Personal communication with Roza Lundina.

2. Personal interviews with Roza Lundina, August 27, 1998, and February 14, 2007.

Chapter 4. Leon Zeeberg

1. Leon Zeeberg, interviewed by Eileen Gottlieb, March 25, 1998, for the Shoah Foundation.
2. Notes from Shira Kafer, informal interview with her grandfather, Leon Zeeberg, January 29, 2008.
3. Gottlieb interview.

Chapter 5. Dora Rytman

1. Mark Wyman, *DPs: Europe's Displaced Persons, 1945–1951* (Ithaca and London: Cornell University Press, 2nd edition, 1998), pp. 140–146.
2. Yehuda Bauer, *Flight and Rescue: Brichah: The Organized Escape of the Jewish Survivors of Eastern Europe, 1944–1948* (New York: Random House, 1970), pp. 114–116.
3. Abraham S. Hyman, *The Undefeated* (Hewlett, N.Y.: Gefen Publishing House, 1993), pp. 181–185.
4. Dora Rytman, "Witness to War: 1941–1945: The Soviet Jewish Experience," Bruce M. Stave (ed.), Betty N. Hoffman (project director and ed.) (Hartford, Conn.: *Connecticut Jewish History, The Journal of the Jewish Historical Society of Greater Hartford*, Summer 2001); Personal interview with Dora Rytman, February 13, 2007.

Chapter 6. The Lazowski Family

1. Combined interviews with Ruth Rabinowitz Lazowski, by Adele Gaster for the Jewish Historical Society of Greater Hartford, June 3, 1994, and Betty N. Hoffman, February 15, 2008.
2. Philip Lazowski, *Faith and Destiny* (Hartford, Conn.: Fox Press, 1975), pp. 40–41.
3. Ibid., p. 82.
4. Personal interview with Philip Lazowski, February 15, 2008.
5. Abraham S. Hyman, *The Undefeated* (Hewlett, N.Y.: Gefen Publishing House, 1993), p. 60.
6. Personal interview with Philip Lazowski, February 15, 2008.
7. Lazowski, pp. 83–84.
8. Ibid., p. 90.

Chapter 7. Henry Levy

1. Henry Levy uses this spelling for Salonica. Others use Salonika or Thessaloniki.
2. Aron Rodrigue, "Sephardim and the Holocaust," United States Holocaust Memorial Museum, Ina Levine Lecture, 2004, pp. 3–8, <http://www.ushmm.org/research/center/publications/occasional/2005-07-01/paper.pdf> (January 11, 2010).
3. "Archbishop Damaskinos and Greek Intellectuals Protest Persecution of Greek Jewry," Jewish Virtual Library, original source at Yad Vashem, *Chronika*, 1984, <http://www.jewishvirtuallibrary.org/jsource/Holocaust/greekbishop.html> (February 24, 2010).
4. "Salonika: Timeline," United States Holocaust Memorial Museum, n.d., <http://www.ushmm.org/wlc/media_cm.php?lang=en&ModuleId=10005422&MediaId=1595> (January 11, 2010).
5. "Auschwitz," United States Holocaust Memorial Museum, May 4, 2009, <http://www.ushmm.org/wlc/article.php?lang=en&ModuleId=10005576> (January 11, 2010).
6. "Warsaw Ghetto Uprising," United States Holocaust Memorial Museum, May 4, 2009, <http://www.ushmm.org/wlc/article.php?ModuleId=10005188> (January 11, 2010).
7. Rodrigue, p. 11.
8. "The Revolt of the Sonderkommando Jews," Let My People Live: The International Forum in Commemoration of the 60th Anniversary of Auschwitz-Birkenau Liberation, May 20, 2008, <http://www.auschwitz.org.pl/new/let_my_people_live/forum/www.auschwitzanniversary2005.pl/index-eng47eb.html?s2=articles&s3=ruch_oporu> (February 17, 2010).
9. "The Holocaust in Greece," United States Holocaust Memorial Museum, n.d., <http://www.ushmm.org/museum/exhibit/online/greece/greece.pdf> (January 11, 2010).
10. Henry Levy, *The Jews of Salonica and the Holocaust: A Personal Memoir* (Unpublished manuscript, the Jewish Historical Society of Greater Hartford, 1991), p. 19.
11. Personal communication with Henry Levy, February 13, 2008.

Chapter 8. Bernard Ostfeld

1. "Italy," United States Holocaust Memorial Museum, May 4, 2009, <http://www.ushmm.org/wlc/article.php?lang=en&ModuleId=10005455> (January 11, 2010).

2. Jane Latus Jones, "Memories of a 'Lucky Jew,'" *The Bloomfield Journal*, Bloomfield, Conn., May 23, 1985, vol. 9, p. 11.

3. Bernard Ostfeld, interview by Gloria Bein, July 31, 1985, for the Jewish Historical Society of Greater Hartford.

Conclusion

1. Mark Wyman, *DPs: Europe's Displaced Persons, 1945–1951* (Ithaca and London: Cornell University Press, 2nd edition, 1998), p. 188.

2. Lottie Rothenberg, "The time the Jews danced through the night in celebration," *Hartford Courant*, May 12, 1987.

3. Wyman, p. 194.

4. President Harry S. Truman, July 25, 1948, in Abraham S. Hyman, *The Undefeated* (Hewlett, N.Y.: Gefen Publishing House, 1993), Appendix VII, p. 473.

5. Leonard Dinnerstein, *America and the Survivors of the Holocaust* (New York: Columbia University Press, 1982), p. 252.

6. Wyman, p. 194.

7. Dinnerstein, p. 252.

8. Wyman, p. 189.

9. Ephriam Dekel, *B'RICHA: Flight to the Homeland* (New York: Herzl Press, 1973), p. 116.

10. Yehuda Bauer, *Out of the Ashes: The Impact of American Jews on Post-Holocaust European Jewry* (Oxford: Pergamon Press, 1989), pp. 220–222.

11. Hyman, p. 435.

12. "Foehrenwald," United States Holocaust Memorial Museum, May 4, 2009, <http://www.ushmm.org/wlc/article.php?lang=en&ModuleId=10007059> (January 11, 2010).

13. Rothenberg, May 12, 1987.

Allies—The collection of nations allied, or joined together, against Germany, Italy, and Japan in World War II. More than forty countries made up the Allies, many joining late in the war. The main Allies were the United States, the United Kingdom (which includes England), the Soviet Union, and France.

antisemitism—Hatred of Jews simply because they are Jews. This hatred may come from religious, political, or economic reasons, and it can lead to prejudice, discrimination, and murder.

crematorium (plural, crematoria)—Facility in which the bodies of people who had been killed in gas chambers were burned.

death camp—A facility designed by the Nazis for mass murder, with gas chambers and crematory ovens.

displaced persons (DP) camp—A temporary home for many people who were living outside their countries after World War II. Germany was divided into four zones (corresponding to the United States, Britain, France, and the Soviet Union). Each country managed the DP camps in its own zone. DP camps were often former schools, apartment buildings, hospitals, or concentration camps.

ghetto—In Nazi Germany, a run-down area in a city or town where Jews were forced to live.

Nazi Party—It began in 1919 as the German Workers' Party. The next year it changed its name to the National Socialist German Workers' Party, a political organization based on principles of extreme nationalism, militarism, racism, and totalitarianism.

partisan—A person belonging to a group of people, often Soviet soldiers and ghetto escapees, who hid from the Nazis and fought them in the forests of the Soviet Union and eastern Poland.

pogrom—A brutal and violent action usually aimed at a particular ethnic or religious group.

Red Army—The nickname for the Soviet Union's army.

Sonderkommando—Special work group assigned to the gas chambers and crematoria.

transit camp—Collecting place, or holding camp, for people who would be sent to other camps, usually death camps.

work camp—A place that housed prisoners who were forced to work for the Nazis under brutal conditions.

Books

Boraks-Nemetz, Lilian and Irene N. Watts, eds. *Tapestry of Hope: Holocaust Writing for Young People*. Plattsburg, N.Y.: Tundra Books of Northern New York, 2003.

Rubin, Susan Goldman. *The Flag With Fifty-Six Stars: A Gift From the Survivors of Mauthausen*. New York: Holiday House, 2005.

Siegal, Aranka. *Grace in the Wilderness: After the Liberation, 1945–1948*. New York: Farrar, Straus and Giroux, 2003.

Smith, Lyn. *Remembering: Voices of the Holocaust: A New History in the Words of the Men and Women Who Survived*. New York: Basic Books, 2007.

Zullo, Allan and Mara Bovsun. *Survivors: True Stories of Children in the Holocaust*. New York: Scholastic, 2004.

Internet Addresses

United States Holocaust Memorial Museum: "Liberation"
   <http://www.ushmm.org/museum/exhibit/focus/liberation/>

USC Shoah Foundation Institute
   <http://college.usc.edu/vhi/>

Yad Vashem, The Holocaust Martyrs' and Heroes' Remembrance Authority
   <http://www.yadvashem.org/>